THREE NIGHTS IN TEHRAN

I0140073

John Strand

BROADWAY PLAY PUBLISHING INC
224 E 62nd St, NY, NY 10065
www.broadwayplaypub.com
info@broadwayplaypub.com

THREE NIGHTS IN TEHRAN
© Copyright 2010 by John Strand

All rights reserved. This work is fully protected under the copyright laws of the United States of America. No part of this publication may be photocopied, reproduced, stored in a retrieval system, or transmitted, in any form or by any means, electronic, mechanical, recording, or otherwise, without the prior permission of the publisher. Additional copies of this play are available from the publisher.

Written permission is required for live performance of any sort. This includes readings, cuttings, scenes, and excerpts. For amateur and stock performances, please contact Broadway Play Publishing Inc. For all other rights contact Bill Craver, Paradigm Agency, 360 Park Avenue S, NY NY 10010, 212 897-6400, wcraver@ paradigmagency.com.

First printing: September 2010
I S B N: 978-0-88145-431-4

Book design: Marie Donovan
Typographic controls: Adobe InDesign
Typeface: Palatino
Printed and bound in the U S A

THREE NIGHTS IN TEHRAN premiered at Signature
Theater in Arlington, Virginia, on 24 November 1996.
The cast and creative contributors were:

OLLIE, *alias* "GOODE"...Bill Mondy
BUD, alias "KELLY" ....Michael Goodwin
GEORGE, *alias* "O'NEILL"....................................Hugh Nees
HOWIE, *alias* "O'REILLY" ....Marty Lodge
AMI, *alias* "PADDY" ....Michael Wikes
DAEMON..Sarah Marshall
GHORBA... Lawrence Redmond
HIGH OFFICIAL ....Kit Halliday

Director... Kyle Donnelly
Set design .... Lou Stancari
Costume design.. Anne Kennedy
Lighting design .... Michele McDermott
Sound design..David Maddox
Properties .... Eleanor Gomberg
Stage manager..Julie A Hunter

CHARACTERS & SETTING

"KELLY", *also known as Bud: former National Security Adviser for the United States of America*

"GOODE", *also known as Ollie: staffer for the National Security Council; officer in the United States Marine Corps*

"O'NEILL", *also known as George: officer in the C I A*

"O'REILLY", *also known as Howie: staffer for the N S C*

"PADDY", *also known as Ami: member of Israeli intelligence*

GHORBA, *expatriate Iranian arms dealer*

HIGH OFFICIAL *of the Iranian government*

LOW OFFICIAL 1

LOW OFFICIAL 2

IRANIAN MAN, *hotel employee*

IRANIAN WOMAN, *hotel employee*

DAEMON

The play requires 7 actors: 6 men, 1 woman. They play a total of 12 roles.

The principle action of the play takes place in a hotel in Tehran, Iran, from Sunday, May 25 to Wednesday, May 29, 1986.

A KEY TO THE HISTORIC FIGURES

KELLY: *Robert McFarlane, former National Security Adviser*

GOODE: *Lieutenant Colonel Oliver L North, N S C*

O'NEILL: *George Cave, C I A*

O'REILLY: *Howard Teicher, N S C*

PADDY: *Amiram Nir, Israeli Intelligence*

GHORBA: *Manucher Ghorbanifar, expatriate Iranian arms dealer*

ACKNOWLEDGMENTS

My thanks to Eric D Schaeffer, Signature Theater's artistic director, and to Marcia Gardner, director of Signature's play development series, "Stages," for their early interest in this play, and their continuous support and encouragement; and to the other members of the Signature team, especially Paul Gamble, managing director, and Ronnie Gunderson, production supervisor. Thanks also to Arena Stage, Washington, DC, which first presented the play to the public as part of its PlayQuest series, with the kind support of Darrl V Jones, associate producer, Cathy Madison, literary manager, and their colleagues. I extend special thanks to the actors who worked with this text in its earlier versions at both Signature and Arena: Sarah Marshall, Marty Lodge, H Michael Walls, David Marks, Jason Kravits, Scott Seder, Angel Torres, Jerry Whiddon, Stan Shulman. And a very special thanks to Kyle Donnelly for her encouragement, her advocacy, and above all her talent, which have combined to make this a far better play than it would have been without her. A heartfelt thank-you to Starr Kopper for her invaluable help and inspiration. And finally, my love and gratitude to Amanda Strand for providing the greater wisdom in all things.

The genius of you Americans is that you never make clear-cut stupid moves, only complicated stupid moves which make us wonder at the possibility that there may be something we are missing.
Gamal Abdel Nasser

We did not—repeat—did not trade weapons or anything else for hostages—nor will we.
President Ronald Reagan
address to the nation
November 13, 1986

...I was upset to hear that possibly—this was through hearsay—that possibly the White House might be taking a position that was fundamentally untrue.
Robert C McFarlane
testimony to the Tower Commission
February 21, 1987

Does Oliver North Tell the Truth?
Title of an article in Reader's Digest, *June, 1993*

North admitted [...] to having participated in the creation of false chronologies to Congress and to having lied to Congress...
Lawrence Walsh, special prosecutor,
Iran-Contra Final Report, 1993

Whenever I tell my kids about my nearly idyllic childhood, I get the feeling that deep down, they suspect that Dad is making the whole thing up.
Oliver North
Under Fire: An American Story

INTRODUCTION

The "world stage." Historians sometimes speak of it with awe, this imagined space where events of great import are played out to our general fascination. The phrase evokes weighty drama—Sophocles, say, or Strindberg. But we are just as likely to witness the occasional satyr play on the world stage. History as *commedia dell'arte* or 17th-century French farce. In the 1980s, the Reagan administration gave the world several marvelous examples.

Of America's foreign policy initiatives launched during the five year period when Marine Lieutenant Colonel Oliver L North was in the employ of the Reagan White House, several vie for the honor of most resembling pages from a Tom Clancy novel—the Grenada invasion, the midair arrest of the *Achille Lauro* hijackers, the secret operation to supply the Nicaraguan Contras in defiance of a Congressional ban. None, however, surpasses the 1986 attempt to trade arms to Iran in exchange for the release of U S hostages held in Beirut.

A few of the facts, now public record, help set the tone. The arms-for-hostages initiative was masterminded by Colonel North. The top-secret American delegation to Iran included North, former National Security Adviser Robert McFarlane, C I A operatives George Cave and Howard Teicher, and Israeli secret agent Amiram Nir: five men highly trained in the selective use of truth, or "lying," as the non-covert world refers to it.

Their Iranian contact was Manucher Ghorbanifar, an Iranian expatriate arms dealer who stood to make several million dollars off the deal. Ghorbanifar was considered by American intelligence to be a cheat, a liar and possibly an Israeli double-agent. He once flunked a C I A lie detector test by answering falsely every question except "What is your name?"

Ghorba, as he was affectionately called by North, was in charge of logistics in Tehran.

The Americans landed in Tehran in an unmarked Israeli military jet. To provide deniability, they carried phony Irish passports and were posing as Irish tourists. They were so thoroughly uninformed about Islamic culture that they arrived during the holy month of Ramadan, when Muslims fast from dawn to dusk.

These were the men entrusted with the first high-level, American-Iranian face-to-face meeting in more than six years. Dependent on their success were four American hostages in Lebanon, America's reputation in international diplomacy (which rested upon a stern warning to other countries never to negotiate with terrorists or deal on any level with "terrorist states"), and—to a degree known only to the feverishly imaginative North—the fate of the Contras in Nicaragua.

Perhaps the stage is, after all, the proper forum for diplomats such as these.

for Amanda

PROLOGUE

(Aboard an unmarked government aircraft, in the early morning hours of Sunday, May 25, 1986. The steady hum of the turbines in the background. Seated before us, alone, is GOODE. *He wears a Marine officer's uniform, a Lieutenant Colonel's, to be exact. He does not speak, but we hear his thoughts)*

GOODE: *(V O)* A silence falls upon the conference room. All the words have now been spoken, all the arguments made. Slowly, he focuses his wise, ancient eyes on me. "Colonel," he says, in that raspy voice, "What do *you* think?" My eyes meet his. I remember the freckle-faced boy I once was. I see again the work-worn eyes of my father. I know that all time has been leading up to this very moment. "Mister President," I say. "The fact is, Sir... Americans are in trouble. They're praying for us to come." His eyes begin to water. Around the table, powerful men clear their throats.

(The CAPTAIN's *voice is heard on the aircraft's intercom system)*

CAPTAIN: *(V O)* Gentlemen, this is your captain speaking.

GOODE: *(V O)* Captain, my captain!

CAPTAIN: *(V O)* We are approaching Iranian airspace. On behalf of the Agency, and the American people, though they shall never know what you do for them this day: good luck. And God be with you.

GOODE: (*V O*) And with your spirit. (*A beat*) I called him "The Old Man." It was a term of endearment. He once put his arm around my shoulder. As a father to a son... Devotion. Sacrifice. Faith. The parallels. A sort of priesthood? Explore this. But watch it. Sort of thing the cynics will tear to pieces...

(*Enter* KELLY, *coming down the aisle. He stops and lays a friendly hand on* GOODE's *shoulder*)

KELLY: Get some sleep, Soldier. (*He exits, back up the aisle.*)

GOODE: (*V O*) Sleep. For the innocent..."Deep in the bombed-out bowels of a Beirut suburb, four American citizens prepared to face another day of physical and mental—" No. Wait. I did that one already. Where am I? *Memoirs of a Freedom Fighter.* Volume One. Chapter Three. May 25, 1986. We were streaking out of Israel, across the Biblical Holy Lands, where the Prophets once strode, where the walls of Jericho came a-tumblin' down. Our destination: the jaws of the lion. Iran. A terrorist nation. Our cargo: sophisticated weaponry— and a presidential mandate to redraw the map of the Middle East." The camera pulls back. The aircraft roars across the screen and disappears into the sun.

(*Enter a woman rather hideously dressed as a little girl: patent leather shoes and white socks, lots of leg, high, ruffled skirt, ribbons in her hair, etc—but also lipstick, heavy eye make-up, etc. This is* GOODE's DAEMON. *She skips down the aisle*)

DAEMON: I'm here, I'm here, I came anyway!

GOODE: Oh, God. Please...

DAEMON: I disobeyed an order. Will you have to spank me?

GOODE: (*Looking away:*) If I don't see her, she doesn't exist.

DAEMON: Of course I exist, Ollie. Deal with it.

GOODE: Voices I could deal with. But visions...

DAEMON: I love your visions. They're so... grandiose.

GOODE: (*Trying not to look at her:*) Please. Leave me alone.

DAEMON: When you're alone, bad things happen. You get carried away.

(*Enter O'NEILL, strolling down the aisle. He cannot see the DAEMON*)

GOODE: (*To DAEMON:*) Just go away!

(DAEMON *hides behind* GOODE's *seat*)

O'NEILL: O K, O K. Don't be so touchy. What are you, nervous? A covert superstar like you? (*He tosses* GOODE *a Hawaiian shirt*) Here. Put this on. You're an Irish tourist, remember?

(*As* O'NEILL *returns up the aisle and exits,* GOODE *holds up the shirt*)

DAEMON: You look good in floral.

GOODE: (*V O*) Into the jaws of the lion? In this?

(*Engine sounds up, lights fade. Stirring music as* DAEMON *wheels* GOODE *off, and they exit*)

DAY ONE, SCENE ONE

(*Sunday, May 25, 1986. A suite in the Independence Hotel, Tehran. The large room is in darkness, but we can make out the central couch and two chairs around a small coffee table; the curtains upstage left that for the moment cover the sliding glass doors to the balcony; the two doors upstage center that lead to the bedrooms; the smaller door upstage right leading to the bathroom; and further downstage, far left, the door leading, apparently, out of the suite.*)

(We can also see a figure on his hands and knees carefully placing a microphone and wires under the couch. When the first sounds off are heard, the figure rises quickly and hides behind the balcony curtains)

VOICES: *(Off)* Dammit.
What is it?
What's the matter?
This key.
What's wrong now?
How do you say "new key"?
We can't get in?
Call someone.
Let me try it.
I'll do it.
Let me try it.
I said I'll do it.

(A few thumps are heard and the door is forced open with a loud snap, as if something is broken. Bright light spills in from the hallway. A beat)

VOICES: *(Off)* Hold it.
Oh, come on.
No, no.
What is this?
Let him go ahead.
The movies?
Sir?

(A beat. GOODE enters the room and halts. He is dressed in tacky, ill-fitting tourist clothes. A small camera hangs from his neck. He withdraws a flashlight from his pocket and sweeps the room with its beam)

VOICES: *(Off)* Can we dispense with the Hollywood?
Let him do his job.

(GOODE settles his light on the large portrait of the Ayatollah Khomeini. A beat, and he switches it off)

GOODE: All clear, Sir.

(*Enter* KELLY, O'REILLY, O'NEILL, *and* PADDY. *They are all carrying suitcases and are dressed in the same tourist clothes, and all have small cameras around their necks. They survey the room.* O'REILLY *seems in a particular hurry, and opens all the doors.* GOODE *continues his security inspection.*)

KELLY: Let's regroup and reassess.

O'NEILL: I don't believe this.

KELLY: No bickering, men.

O'REILLY: Where's the latrine!?

KELLY: In this together.

O'REILLY: (*Finding the bathroom*) Oh, God!

(O'REILLY *enters, shuts the door*)

O'NEILL: Inspector Clouseau at the Tehran Hilton.

PADDY: Now Hotel Istiqlal. "Independence."

KELLY: All right. Who has the cake and the guns?

O'NEILL: Did you see those goons in the hallway?

GOODE: Chief?

PADDY: Revolutionary Guards.

GOODE: Chief?

KELLY: Do you have the cake?

PADDY: We are trapped here. You realize this?

KELLY: Or the guns?

GOODE: Chief?

KELLY: What is it?

GOODE: Suggest you take the east room, Sir. It's the most secure.

O'NEILL: Secure like a snake pit.

KELLY: Hold it. I have the cake. Somebody else has the guns.

(Unseen by any of the new arrivals, the figure slips out from behind the balcony curtain and exits through the open door)

PADDY: Microphones everywhere. Also cameras.

KELLY: Where's Howie?

PADDY: Darkness at noon. Trust no one.

(PADDY pulls the chord on the curtains and the balcony is revealed. Daylight fills the suite. There is a view of the mountains in the distance. A beat, as they stare)

O'NEILL: Nice view.

KELLY: Howie?

PADDY: The Elburz Mountains.

GOODE: Suggest we do a quick inventory, Chief.

(When no one is looking, a figure sneaks across the balcony and out of sight)

KELLY: Did Howie come up with us?

O'NEILL: The Guards kept our passports, you know.

GOODE: Negative.

O'NEILL: Check your pockets.

(GOODE checks his pockets for his passport. O'REILLY, looking pale, emerges from the bathroom, and shuts the door)

O'REILLY: Don't go in there.

KELLY: Do you have the guns?

O'REILLY: Smells like something died.

PADDY: Yes. Democracy.

GOODE: Sir, the passports have been confiscated.

O'REILLY: How do you say "plumbing problem" in Farsi?

KELLY: (*Looking through his suitcase*) Dammit. I was sure I had the guns.

O'NEILL: Does that mean I can stop playing an Irish tourist?

GOODE: Negative. Maintain cover.

PADDY: Irish tourist does not say "negative".

GOODE: Roger.

O'NEILL: They don't say "Roger", either.

KELLY: Men. Regroup. Reassess.

PADDY: Irish tourists. Who will believe this?

O'NEILL: Ask James Bond here.

PADDY: No Irish in Islamic country. You cannot drink.

KELLY: All right. Quick inventory. I have the cake. Who has the Bible?

GOODE: I do, Sir.

KELLY: Howie?

O'REILLY: Yes, Sir.

KELLY: What is that smell?

GOODE: Sir, the guns were assigned to O'Neill.

KELLY: Who's O'Neill? Is that you, Ami?

PADDY: I am Paddy.

O'NEILL: I'm O'Neill.

KELLY: I thought you were O'Reilly.

O'REILLY: I'm O'Reilly, Sir.

KELLY: Well, who am I?

O'NEILL: You're Kelly, Sir.

KELLY: Good.

GOODE: Yes, Sir?

KELLY: What?

GOODE: William P. Goode, Dublin, Ireland.

KELLY: Where's my passport?

O'REILLY: Guys?

GOODE: Revolutionary Guards have it, Sir.

KELLY: What!?

O'REILLY: Guys, you know the tap water at the airport?

GOODE: Confiscated them all, Sir.

O'REILLY: Avoid it.

KELLY: Why wasn't I informed? George.

O'NEILL: What, Sir?

KELLY: If I have the cake, you should have the guns.

O'NEILL: Got 'em, Sir.

PADDY: What is that stench?

KELLY: O K. Ollie?

GOODE: It's Goode, Sir.

O'NEILL: Not so good if you ask me.

KELLY: Roger. Rough start. Pushed around by those damn punks with the AK-47s.

GOODE: Suggest we maintain cover, everybody?

O'NEILL: They treated us like Irish tourists.

GOODE: For security reasons?

KELLY: No delegation, no motorcade.

PADDY: No one even to meet our plane.

GOODE: This whole suite could be bugged.

O'REILLY: They didn't even know we were coming.

PADDY: It is bugged. They know we are here.

O'NEILL: I think I see a pattern.

KELLY: Howie?

O'REILLY: Sir?

KELLY: Regroup and reassess. Verify our list of, uh—
Howie, where's my, where's my—?

O'REILLY: Pocket, Sir.

KELLY: Found it. Items. Ollie?

O'NEILL: How about we try to get a little breakfast
first?

KELLY: Negative. Ollie.

GOODE: One kosher chocolate cake, check. Twin set of
pearl-handled .357 magnums, check.

KELLY: Hold it. Arabs eat kosher?

GOODE: Negative.

O'NEILL: We bought the cake in Tel Aviv before we
left.

PADDY: Best in Israel. Baker is cousin to me.

O'NEILL: That explains the price.

PADDY: Hey.

GOODE: Bible with inscription from RR, check. Irish
passports confiscated.

KELLY: Check.

PADDY: And they take the parts.

KELLY: What?

PADDY: From off the airplane.

KELLY: Whole pallet of spare parts? Ollie?

GOODE: Roger. But we've still got the satellite photos.

KELLY: Well, thank God for that. Who's got them?

(A beat as everyone searches his pockets, suitcase, etc.)

O'REILLY: Sir?

KELLY: What is it?

O'REILLY: Request permission to call room maintenance.

KELLY: Permission delayed. Listen up, everybody. O K. Off to a bad start. No getting frazzled. Too much at stake. Need to work as a team. I want cooperation. I want execution. Problems come up, the buck stops with me. Understood?

ALL: Yes, Sir.

KELLY: All right. Progress assessment. George.

O'NEILL: We're stuck on the fifteenth floor of a hotel full of armed guards in a hostile city at war.

PADDY: And we are unarmed.

O'REILLY: And the plumbing's backed up.

KELLY: Hold it. Almost forgot: the pills. Everybody verify. Where's my—?

O'REILLY: Pocket, Sir.

KELLY: Got 'em. Not pleasant. Take your own life. Keep 'em close at hand. If things get rough, interrogation and so forth—

O'REILLY: Sir? Those are your Valium.

KELLY: Oh. Well, where are my—?

O'REILLY: Pocket, Sir.

GOODE: Sir. Can we go over the agenda?

O'NEILL: How about the menu, then the agenda?

KELLY: Roger, Ollie. Go ahead.

GOODE: Today, Sunday, 25 May. Twelve hundred hours: First meeting with top Iranians, probably the Prime Minister and/or the Speaker of Parliament. They should be here any minute. We deliver the first load of HAWK missile parts.

KELLY, O'NEILL, PADDY & O'REILLY: Whoa, whoa. Hold it. Wait a minute (*etc.*)

O'NEILL: They already took the parts.

GOODE: Right. OK, delivery made. Fourteen hundred hours: release of first American hostages in Beirut. Fourteen hundred-oh-five: the second plane with the rest of the HAWKs and TOW anti-tank shells takes off from Israel, headed for Bandar Abbas, Iran.

PADDY: So: arms for hostages.

KELLY: Negative. Howie?

O'REILLY: The weapons are a concrete gesture of good faith, in no way linked to human American lives.

PADDY: Ha! If you don't have back your hostages, what?

KELLY: Howie?

O'REILLY: Well... Ollie?

GOODE: Our gesture is planned to result in their gesture.

PADDY: One gesture, arms. Other gesture, hostage. What is difference?

KELLY: Let's not split semantic hairs, O K? Ollie.

GOODE: Twenty-hundred hours: Working dinner with top aides of the Prime Minister and the Speaker. I give them the maps and the satellite photos, and brief them on Iraqi and Soviet troop positions.

KELLY: Good.

GOODE: What, Sir?

KELLY: No, go ahead.

GOODE: Twenty-four-hundred hours: Release of remaining American hostages. Suggest we keep Monday night open for dinner with the Ayatollah.

KELLY: Dinner Khomeini. Roger. Beautiful. I'll want photos. Howie, make a note. Questions.

PADDY: Do you think you are in Disneyland?

KELLY: Fair enough. Ollie?

PADDY: Iranians I know. Horse thieves and murderers. We are trapped here. Our lives, in the hands of madmen. I am warning you: Trust no one.

(*A knock at the door*)

GOODE: They're here! Everybody: Look sharp! O'Reilly, O'Neill, get rid of those suitcases. Paddy: I know what you Israelis think of American intelligence. But just watch us this time.

(GOODE *opens the door. A bearded man, dressed simply but neatly, and a young woman wearing a chador stand in the hallway.* GOODE *leads them in*)

GOODE: (*Extending his hand*) Come in. We are honored. Come in, please. (*Ceremoniously*) On behalf of the President of the United States of America: welcome to this historic opportunity. May I present to you my superior, head of our National Security Council?

KELLY: An historic honor.

(GOODE *has led the Iranians to the couch, where he seats them.*)

GOODE: We come in peace. We are here to break new ground. Sir?

KELLY: In the name of the President, the people, the spirit of democracy, let me say: new dawn. Your revolution: it's yours, fine, you can have it. But the very fact that you are sitting here, right here. It's...

O'REILLY: Historic.

KELLY: Historic. And now: tokens. Howie?

O'REILLY: The following are gifts from the government of the United States of America as a gesture of renewed understanding. One pair of collector's quality .357 magnum handguns.

(The two Iranians accept the gifts in silent amazement)

KELLY: Not for use on us!

(Forced laughter all around)

O'REILLY: One cake, chocolate, decorated with a symbolic brass key.

GOODE: We'll all have a piece when the hostages are free.

KELLY: Accept these token gestures, understanding.

(A beat)

IRANIAN MAN: *(With a heavy accent:)* What do you want?

KELLY: New dawn.

GOODE: And the hostages.

KELLY: Roger. Together, let us break new ground.

IRANIAN WOMAN: What you break goes on bill. Hotel rules.

IRANIAN MAN: No food.

IRANIAN WOMAN: Until dark. It is for us holy month Ramadan.

(A beat. The Americans look at one another)

O'NEILL: Who are you?

IRANIAN MAN: Room Service.

O'NEILL: They're Room Service.

GOODE: O K, there's a miscommunication here.

O'NEILL: I think I see a pattern.

(PADDY *and* O'NEILL *take their suitcases and exit to bedroom.*)

KELLY: Ollie. I want to see you in my room.

(KELLY *exits to bedroom.*)

GOODE: Yes, Sir. (*Herding the two* IRANIAN *out*) O K, let's clear the room.

O'REILLY: Ollie: the gifts!

GOODE: Wait a minute, you two. Give me those.

(*They don't wish to give them back*)

GOODE: That's Irish government property. (*He is forced to pull them from their hands.*) Miscommunication! We're simple Irish tourists—! Give it here!

O'REILLY: (*Rushing urgently to the door, gripping* IRANIAN MAN's *arm:*) Wait! Listen to me carefully: Do you fix plumbing? Do you fix plumbing?

IRANIAN MAN: (*To his companion*) Madmen!

(*Exit* IRANIAN MAN *and* WOMAN. *Lights down. Music and the rising sound of an angry street mob chanting in Farsi*)

DAY ONE, SCENE TWO

(GOODE, O'NEILL, O'REILLY *seated in postures of tense boredom around the coffee table.* GOODE *occupies one of the chairs*)

O'REILLY: All afternoon?

O'NEILL: All afternoon.

GOODE: In the desert heat?

O'NEILL: Under the searing desert sun.

O'REILLY: Old men? Old women?

O'NEILL: And children. And cripples.

(Enter KELLY, *without trousers, crossing)*

KELLY: Can't seem to find my, uh— Anyone seen my, uh—? *(He exits back to bedroom.)*

O'NEILL: On the ninth day of the Hajj, the whole Plain of Arafat, covered with worshippers standing— *standing*—in prayer.

O'REILLY: Whoa.

O'NEILL: Not kneeling in an air-conditioned church with reserved parking for your B M W.

O'REILLY: Amazing.

O'NEILL: Reading the Koran and calling out, "Here I am, O Lord!"

GOODE: Good way to die from sunstroke.

O'NEILL: They'd welcome death: they go straight to paradise.

(Re-enter KELLY.)

KELLY: Gray pinstripes? Go with my good suit, can't figure out— *(He exits back into bedroom.)*

O'NEILL: Total commitment. Christianity has nothing to equal it.

GOODE: Religious fanatics.

O'NEILL: Admit it, Ollie: you're jealous. Islam is young, strong and hungry. By comparison, Christianity is a dried-out corpse.

GOODE: You ever hear Billy Graham speak?

O'NEILL: In the Astrodome. Five-dollar hotdogs, twenty-dollar tee-shirts.

O'REILLY: Jim Bakker's good.

O'NEILL: What?

O'REILLY: Jim and Tammie Bakker?

O'NEILL: Pain, martyrdom, holy wars. When was the last time you saw an Episcopalian whip himself bloody in public? You're in Virginia holding bake sales. The future belongs to the Moslems. They'll drink your Christian blood.

GOODE: They'd lose a hell of a lot before they got any of *this* blood.

O'REILLY: Don't let him bait you, Ollie.

O'NEILL: They'll spread their prayer mats on the White House lawn.

GOODE: Desert heat's getting to *you*, George.

O'NEILL: Your granddaughters will wear chadors and carry the Koran to school.

GOODE: I'll put my money on God the Father versus Allah any day of the week.

O'NEILL: Can't: they're the same god.

O'REILLY: Really?

O'NEILL: Read the Koran: it's got Noah, Moses, Abraham. God got fed up with the Christians and the Jews, so he revealed his word to Mohammed beginning in 610 A D. We call him God, Moslems call him Allah. Simple as that.

GOODE: Got all the answers, don't you, George.

O'NEILL: You'd make a good Moslem fundamentalist, Ollie. No separation of church and state. Women suppressed. All stuff you believe in.

O'REILLY: Guys? Come on. What time is it?

O'NEILL: Five minutes later than the last time you asked.

(*Re-enter* KELLY, *crossing.*)

KELLY: Ollie. Getting late.

GOODE: Yes, Sir.

KELLY: Ollie. (*He motions for* GOODE *to join him downstage, aside*) Lot riding.

GOODE: Sir?

KELLY: On this.

GOODE: Right.

KELLY: Stay with me?

GOODE: Sir?

KELLY: The men. Morale. That sort of thing.

GOODE: Yes, Sir.

KELLY: You, me. Disagreements.

GOODE: Sir?

KELLY: Not personal. Policy.

GOODE: Right.

KELLY: Damn policy.

GOODE: I know.

KELLY: Gets between a man and his, his, his—

GOODE: Yes, Sir.

KELLY: No hard feelings.

GOODE: None, no.

KELLY: Because united we stand.

GOODE: Roger. Totally.

KELLY: I like you. Ollie?

GOODE: Sir.

KELLY: That's why, whenever I could—

GOODE: Grateful.

KELLY: Even when they said to me, "Bud, what are you—?"

GOODE: Aware of that.

KELLY: And I'd say, "Hey, look."

GOODE: Appreciate it.

KELLY: Right to their faces, I said, "Hey, look." Because Ollie?

GOODE: Sir.

KELLY: If I had a son.

GOODE: Yes, Sir.

KELLY: Seriously. (*A beat. Suddenly, with exuberance:*) We're gonna do it!

GOODE: Right.

KELLY: Right? Mission accomplished and pow!

GOODE: "Pow."

(*Chuckles*)

KELLY: Future. You've got one.

GOODE: We all, all of us—

KELLY: Me, no.

GOODE: Bud.

KELLY: I'm out of favor.

GOODE: You're here.

KELLY: Face it.

GOODE: They sent you.

KELLY: A last hurrah.

GOODE: New beginning. Bud. You? After everything?

KELLY: You think? Really?

GOODE: I do.

KELLY: You, though. That's what they're saying.

GOODE: Who?

KELLY: Some of them. You could be so— If you just—

GOODE: What?

KELLY: None of this—

GOODE: What?

KELLY: Over the fence, out of the corral and through the woods, you follow me?

GOODE: No.

KELLY: Tight rein. Keep one.

GOODE: Right.

KELLY: By the book and so on.

GOODE: Sure. Yes, Sir.

KELLY: None of this, you know.

GOODE: Don't worry.

KELLY: Because that's where it all stems from.

GOODE: You're right.

KELLY: Am I right?

GOODE: You're right.

(*A beat*)

KELLY: Ollie, can I—? I don't— I'm not— I don't—

GOODE: Look, Bud—

KELLY: (*Rapidly*) Sometimes at night I hold Jonda in my arms so tight that I almost cut off her breathing and she has to wake me to keep from suffocating and I think, God help me, I'm becoming dangerous to the people I love most.

(*A beat*)

GOODE: Bud—

KELLY: I'm sorry—

GOODE: Look—

KELLY: I'm sorry. O K? (*A beat*) Ollie? (*A beat*) Jesus, Ollie!

GOODE: Sure.

KELLY: I didn't mean that.

GOODE: We didn't talk.

KELLY: You mean it?

GOODE: Conversation never took place.

KELLY: No, it didn't, did it? Thanks, Soldier. Friends?

(*Chuckles.* KELLY *turns back to address the others*)

KELLY: George. Background. This Ramadama festival.

O'NEILL: "Ramadan", Sir. The ninth month of the Islamic lunar calendar. Moslems fast from first light to last light. No food or drink, no smoking, no sex.

O'REILLY: A whole month?

GOODE: Wouldn't be that tough.

O'NEILL: An all-day fast makes people very irritable. Probably the worst possible time for negotiation.

KELLY: Good background. Damn hungry. (*He exits into bedroom.*)

O'REILLY: You hungry, Ollie?

GOODE: No.

O'NEILL: He's into fasting. It's like gastronomic push-ups.

GOODE: You think about hamburgers. I think about our people being tortured in Beirut.

O'NEILL: Well, that'll kill your appetite, all right.

GOODE: I'd fast until Christmas if it would bring home one single American hostage.

O'NEILL: Tell me something: Why is it you reduce even complicated international conflicts to the personal level?

GOODE: I care. Simple as that.

O'REILLY: We all care.

O'NEILL: But we don't all take it personally. What is it you said about Abu Nidal?

O'REILLY: George, why don't you give it a rest?

O'NEILL: "I'll take him on anywhere he wants, one-on-one." International diplomacy reduced to a game of pick-up basketball.

O'REILLY: I don't think he meant basketball.

O'NEILL: He outscores Abu Nidal and terrorists all over the globe have to turn in their AK-47s—or else they get a technical foul.

O'REILLY: George.

O'NEILL: What a fantasy. Ever think of starting your own country, Ollie?

GOODE: Yeah. I'd keep out all the loud-mouth, brown-nose bureaucrats.

O'NEILL: And the press. And the opposition. You should stay in Iran.

O'REILLY: That's enough, George.

GOODE: Let him run his mouth. I don't care. Doesn't bother me.

(GOODE *leans in a position of exaggerated nonchalance. The arm of his chair suddenly snaps off, and he nearly falls. Loud laughter from* O'NEILL *and* O'REILLY. GOODE, *holding the arm of the chair, stands over* O'NEILL.)

GOODE: Don't ever mock me, George. Mock me and your days are numbered.

(DAEMON *opens the hall door and steps in quickly*)

DAEMON: Spank him, Ollie! Spank him good!

(GOODE *turns, takes a few steps towards her. Exit* DAEMON *quickly, closing the door.* GOODE, *confused, turns back to his colleagues while still brandishing his "club". Re-enter* KELLY *from the bedrooms to catch* GOODE *in a primitive, war-like posture*)

KELLY: Ollie, dammit. Clowning around. American nationals, tortured in Beirut. That'll go on the bill, Soldier.

(Exit KELLY *into bedroom)*

O'NEILL: You're showing some strain, "Soldier". Why don't you relax and tell us one of your stories about the mutilated war orphans in Central America.

O'REILLY: George.

O'NEILL: Phase One of the Tehran Master Plan is four-and-a-half hours off schedule. Looks like 'History' got stuck in traffic.

GOODE: They'll be here.

O'NEILL: Maybe your Man in Iran ran into trouble.

O'REILLY: Who is he, Ollie?

GOODE: A highly placed source.

O'NEILL: Dinner with the Ayatollah? Must be real high up.

O'REILLY: He better be. He can make or break this whole show.

O'NEILL: If he ever shows up.

GOODE: He's a major player. Knowledge, access and—top of the list—discretion. With him on board...we redraw the map of the Middle East.

(The door swings open and in strolls a portly, Falstaffian figure overdressed in expensive but tasteless clothes. He sports a goatee intended to camouflage a generous double chin. He throws open his arms)

GHORBA: American friends! Let's to making history!

(Lights to black. Iranian music)

DAY ONE, SCENE THREE

(Seated on the couch are two Iranian negotiators, LOW OFFICIAL 1 and LOW OFFICIAL 2. Standing nearby is GHORBA. Downstage center, huddled in conference, are KELLY and GOODE)

KELLY: Ollie, dammit.

GOODE: I know.

KELLY: What the hell is this?

GOODE: Miscommunication.

KELLY: What?

GOODE: Down the line somewhere.

KELLY: Where?

GOODE: I'll fix it.

KELLY: It's our asses.

GOODE: I know.

KELLY: Three solid hours, going nowhere.

GOODE: I know.

KELLY: Who are these jerks?

GOODE: I know, I know.

KELLY: Flunkies. Gophers. Where are the top dogs? Can't talk with these clowns.

GOODE: I'll fix it.

KELLY: "Fix it" how?

GHORBA: My friends. Now to recontinue negotiation. Again I translate.

(KELLY *and* GOODE *return to the group*)

KELLY: Let me see if I've got this straight. You expect us to apologize for past American "sins," as you call them?

GHORBA: (*Translating*) We apologize for our American sins. Sorry.

KELLY: By shipping you another five thousand antitank shells?

GHORBA: (*Translating*) And we send you five thousand shells.

KELLY: You've got to be joking, Pal.

GHORBA: (*Translating*) We do so with good humor.

KELLY: You two are really starting to piss me off.

GHORBA: (*Translating*) I feel an urge to urinate.

KELLY: You have any idea who you're dealing with here?

GHORBA: (*Translating*) Let me introduce myself.

GOODE: This man is my country's national security adviser.

KELLY: I am a cabinet minister.

GOODE: In two years, this man will be president.

KELLY: Ollie.

GOODE: Or a senator. You never thought about it, Bud?

KELLY: Run for office?

GOODE: Why not?

KELLY: I'm a soldier, basically.

GOODE: Senate seat from Virginia? I'd vote for you.

KELLY: No. You would?

GOODE: "The Man Who Freed The American Hostages."

GHORBA: *(To the Iranians)* Domestic politics. Untranslatable.

LOW OFFICIAL 1: *(To his colleague)* Who are these clowns?

LOW OFFICIAL 2: They send us bureaucrats.

LOW OFFICIAL 1: We can't talk with these fools. Give us somebody who can make decisions.

GHORBA: *(To the Americans)* Domestic politics. Untranslatable.

LOW OFFICIAL 1: *(To the Americans)* The evils of war force us to deal with Satan.

GHORBA: *(Translating)* Times are tough.

LOW OFFICIAL 2: Basically, we think you are lower than a snake that crawls through the dust.

GHORBA: *(Translating)* I find you very down-to-earth.

LOW OFFICIAL 1: To us, your whole society is not equal to the scum that floats on a pond full of camel shit.

GHORBA: *(Translating)* You have done wonders controlling water pollution.

LOW OFFICIAL 2: We hate you, we mistrust you, and we spit on your values.

GHORBA: *(Translating)* So let's be friends.

GOODE: If you want more tank shells, what about the hostages in Beirut?

GHORBA: *(Translating)* American hostages.

GOODE: When can you get our people out?

GHORBA: *(Translating)* Any information?

LOW OFFICIAL 1: Hopeless situation.

LOW OFFICIAL 2: Impossibly complicated.

LOW OFFICIAL 1: Allah himself would have a hard time.

GHORBA: (*To the Americans*) With God's help, anything is possible.

KELLY: Then let's have some action.

GOODE: I've spent months hammering out a timetable.

KELLY: We broke our butts to get this far.

GHORBA: (*Translating*) I may have injured my buttocks region.

GOODE: We want our people out.

KELLY: Now.

GOODE: Not a single bullet until we see some hostages.

GHORBA: (*Translating*) Arms for hostages.

LOW OFFICIAL 1: So send us the missiles we paid for.

LOW OFFICIAL 2: And more tank shells.

LOW OFFICIAL 1: And we'll send a delegation to Beirut.

LOW OFFICIAL 2: In a month or two, we'll have some news.

GHORBA: (*Translating*) It may take a few days. Meanwhile, could you spare few more weapons? As humanitarian gesture?

KELLY: (*Losing it*) I have come all the damn way from the United States of America!

GHORBA: (*Translating*) It was a very long flight.

KELLY: I am not some flunky like you. In two years, I could be one of the most powerful senators in Washington.

GHORBA: (*Translating*) I see a career for myself in politics.

KELLY: So listen up, Jokers: either you give us what we came for, or we get back on that plane and we are gone, zip, outta here, get it?

(*From the bedroom, enter* O'REILLY, *with earphones around his neck*)

O'REILLY: Sir. They took our pilot.

KELLY: What!?

O'REILLY: Forcibly removed him. And they refuse to refuel the plane. We could be stuck here.

LOW OFFICIAL 1: (*Standing and withdrawing a piece of paper*) And now: a list of American criminal acts committed under the Shah.

KELLY: Get those two assholes out of my hotel room!

(*Lights to black. Music*)

DAY ONE, SCENE FOUR

(*Lights back up to the same setting, several hours later, early evening, Present are the* LOW OFFICIALS 1 *and* 2, GHORBA, GOODE, *and* O'NEILL. *The fatigue now shows more prominently on each individual*)

GHORBA: They would like a show in faith.

O'NEILL: A what?

GHORBA: A gesture.

O'NEILL: After five-and-a-half hours?

GOODE: I am standing here. That's a gesture.

LOW OFFICIAL 1: Six years.

GHORBA: Six years of war.

LOW OFFICIAL 2: Holy War. We were attacked.

GHORBA: Iraqi aggressors.

O'NEILL: We're officially neutral.

GHORBA: "Neutral." What is this?

LOW OFFICIAL 1: Iraqis have Soviet weapons.

GOODE: How about giving us back our Irish passports?

LOW OFFICIAL 2: We are fighting for our lives.

O'NEILL: You talk about 'gesture.'

GHORBA: Russians on that side—

GOODE: Guys worked hard on those documents.

GHORBA: —why not Americans on this side?

GOODE: I want them back.

LOW OFFICIAL 1: We have suffered.

LOW OFFICIAL 2: Tremendous losses.

LOW OFFICIAL 1: The dead and crippled.

LOW OFFICIAL 2: We can't even count them.

O'NEILL: Look at the time. Is there any reason why we can't get, say, an egg salad sandwich?

LOW OFFICIAL 1: A few missile parts—

LOW OFFICIAL 2: A radar or two—

O'NEILL: Or even a garden salad?

GHORBA: These men could be killed just for coming here.

(The DAEMON appears to GOODE. The others cannot see her)

DAEMON: Give me what I want or I'll scream.

GOODE: (Alarmed:) No!

DAEMON: I'll throw a tantrum!

GOODE: No, don't!

O'NEILL: Ollie?

GOODE: (*To the* DAEMON) What is it you want?

GHORBA: The weapons we paid for!

DAEMON: Chocolate cake.

GOODE: The cake?

O'NEILL: What?

GOODE: Get the cake!

O'NEILL: Right. Good idea.

(O'NEILL *grabs the box with the cake in it, places it on the coffee table, opens it, and stands back.* DAEMON *hovers in the background.*)

GHORBA: What is this?

LOW OFFICIAL 1: What is this?

O'NEILL: Cake.

LOW OFFICIAL 2: It's a trick.

LOW OFFICIAL 1: They're trying to weaken us.

O'NEILL: God, I could eat that whole thing in one bite.

GHORBA: It looks so good.

O'NEILL: No silverware. We'll just take handfuls of it.

GOODE: George. Hold it.

O'NEILL: "Hold it"?

GOODE: Offer them some.

GHORBA: What flavor?

O'NEILL: Why?

GOODE: Basic American table manners.

LOW OFFICIAL 1: It looks like Israeli chocolate kosher.

LOW OFFICIAL 2: Are they crazy?

O'NEILL: Help yourselves, you guys. Dig in.

GHORBA: (*To* O'NEILL) Just medium piece for me, please.

LOW OFFICIAL 1: Ghorba. Don't touch that Jewish shit.

GHORBA: Why?

LOW OFFICIAL 2: How do we know it's not poisoned?

GHORBA: "Poisoned"?

DAEMON: Poisoned? I'm not hungry anymore. (*Exits*)

GOODE: (*To* LOW OFFICIALS) Go ahead. After you.

LOW OFFICIAL 1: These are C I A. Tell him to eat first.

GHORBA: He says, after you.

O'NEILL: Look, I'll start.

GOODE: No. No sign of weakness. If they don't need any, neither do we.

O'NEILL: I need some, I am starving—!

GOODE: No.

GHORBA: (*To* LOW OFFICIAL 1) I offer myself, as guinea lamb.

LOW OFFICIAL 1: No.

LOW OFFICIAL 2: You see how they don't dare to eat first?

LOW OFFICIAL 1: The bastards. Trying to poison us.

GHORBA: Rich, creamy chocolate—

GOODE: Put it away, George.

O'NEILL: Just a really small slice.

GOODE: Put it away, George.

GHORBA: Melting in your mouth—

O'NEILL: One tiny little piece.

GOODE: Unified front.

O'NEILL: A couple of damn crumbs.

GOODE: No signs of weakness.

O'NEILL: Let me lick the frosting.

GOODE: Maintain discipline.

O'NEILL: I need some of that fucking cake!

GOODE: Put it away!! Put it away!! Put it away!!!

(*A beat. Silence.* O'NEILL *reluctantly obeys.*)

LOW OFFICIAL 1: Psychopaths.

LOW OFFICIAL 2: They sent us psychopaths.

GHORBA: Rich, creamy chocolate... This was cheap trick of torture!

GOODE: Ghorba, who's side are you on?

O'NEILL: His.

GHORBA: Whose?

O'NEILL: Your own.

GHORBA: Same as yours, Mister Big American Intelligence Nothing.

GOODE: All right, all right.

O'NEILL: You're on the side of your twenty percent commission.

GHORBA: Fifteen percent, Mister Do Not Have The Facts.

LOW OFFICIAL 1: Never mind these idiot cake tricks! Give us five thousand tank shells.

LOW OFFICIAL 2: We're not asking for Manhattan.

GOODE: Can we get back to the hostages?

(*The following lines are spoken simultaneously:*)

LOW OFFICIAL 1: We already paid you fifteen million dollars, where is our equipment?

LOW OFFICIAL 2: We're risking our necks talking to enemies of the Islamic Republic of Iran—

O'NEILL: Our intelligence shows that they are under your influence, so use it—

GHORBA: I am international businessman. This is humanitarian deal—

GOODE: All right, everybody just relax!

LOW OFFICIAL 1: Question.

GHORBA: Question.

GOODE: I'll answer as honestly as I can. Go ahead.

LOW OFFICIAL 1: What is that disgusting smell?

GOODE: Translation.

GHORBA: Forget it.

(Again, simultaneously:)

LOW OFFICIAL 1: We keep our word, and if you would just keep yours, we wouldn't have this problem—

LOW OFFICIAL 2: All we ask is simple justice, a business deal, same as any other, just look at it that way—

GOODE: What about innocent American citizens in Beirut, what about their families, their loved ones—

(Lights down. Music)

DAY ONE, SCENE FIVE

(Same setting, late that night. GOODE on the couch in his undershirt. On the coffee table before him are various documents, maps, etc. He flips through a notebook, scribbling, crossing things out, etc. He is alone for the moment.

(Silently, a bedroom door opens slowly. It is O'NEILL, in pajamas. He peers out suspiciously at GOODE, as if spying

on him. GOODE *raises his head, looks left.* O'NEILL *slips back into his room, closes the door quietly. A beat.*

(Silently, the other bedroom door opens slowly. It is KELLY, *in pajamas. He peers out suspiciously at* GOODE, *as if spying on him.* GOODE *raises his head, looks right.* KELLY slips back into his room, closes the door quietly. A *beat.*

(Silently, both doors open simultaneously: O'NEILL *and* KELLY, *spying. They see one another and—still silent—try to cover-up, as if all is normal: a friendly nod, a wave, etc.*

(Suddenly O'REILLY, *in his pajamas, emerges from the bathroom, holding a towel over his mouth. He quickly shuts the door behind him.* O'NEILL *and* KELLY *slip quickly back into their rooms and close the doors)*

O'REILLY: I don't know if I can stand that for two more days. (*A beat*) Ollie, don't you want to get some sleep?

GOODE: What's a little stench?

O'REILLY: You didn't sleep last night either.

GOODE: Compared to our people in Beirut? Or Nicaragua?

O'REILLY: Nicaragua?

GOODE: You think *they're* sleeping?

O'REILLY: Who?

GOODE: The people who got us here.

O'REILLY: You got us here.

GOODE: What's the biggest threat we face, Howie?

O'REILLY: From where?

GOODE: That's what I'm asking.

O'REILLY: I don't know, Congress?

GOODE: Global threat.

O'REILLY: Oh. The Soviets, I guess. With the new guy, though—

GOODE: Who?

O'REILLY: Things could change.

GOODE: Things won't change, Howie. Look at me. Right here. Things. Won't. Change. It's optimists like you. We let our guard down, and boom.

O'REILLY: I'm not an optimist.

GOODE: Islam.

O'REILLY: Huh?

GOODE: Religious extremists with a stranglehold on policy. Waving prayer books, telling people they can believe this, they can't believe that.

O'REILLY: (*Chuckling*) Sounds like most of the Republicans I know.

GOODE: What is that, a joke?

O'REILLY: Ollie.

GOODE: That's funny?

O'REILLY: Lighten up a little.

GOODE: Now? Here?

O'REILLY: I'd love to get out. See the city.

GOODE: The jaws of the lion.

O'REILLY: I wish I could speak the language.

GOODE: The gathering storm.

O'REILLY: Talk to the guy in the street. That's how you learn things.

GOODE: They'd tear you apart.

O'REILLY: It's a big city. Six million people.

GOODE: Against one. Bad odds.

O'REILLY: They can't all be fundamentalists.

GOODE: Can't they?

O'REILLY: Shopkeepers, taxi drivers, school kids. People everywhere want the same things, basically.

GOODE: We're rudderless, Howie. I hope you know that.

O'REILLY: "Rudderless"?

GOODE: No leadership.

O'REILLY: There's Bud.

GOODE: That's what I'm saying. Men crack. I saw it in combat. He told me something. His wife. He tried to choke her.

O'REILLY: Bud did?

GOODE: Keep it to yourself.

O'REILLY: Actually choke her?

GOODE: If things unravel, Howie. Somebody's got to take the wheel.

O'REILLY: What wheel?

GOODE: Let me put it this way: I'm in the jungle near the Salvadoran border. We approach a re-supply village. Totally silent. Not a sound except flies, thousands of flies. I know what to expect. We drag the bodies out of the huts. Then I see the little boy, maybe nine or ten, still alive. The face of an angel. His left foot, chopped right off by the Sandanistas. I hold him in my arms. He whispers in my ear: "One favor, Señor, please." What is it, Son? I ask. "Your gun. Let me fight back. Please. For my people."

(A long beat)

O'REILLY: The arm.

GOODE: What?

O'REILLY: The last time you told that story, they chopped off the kid's arm.

GOODE: Do you sleep?

O'REILLY: What?

GOODE: At night?

O'REILLY: Yeah.

GOODE: You trust. You're innocent.

O'REILLY: I'm not innocent.

GOODE: The world's full of simple people, right? With simple desires.

O'REILLY: O K, Ollie—

GOODE: The world I want my kids to live in. Then I think: Jenco, Anderson, Jacobsen, Sutherland. Bill Buckley's body.

O'REILLY: Look, all I said was—

GOODE: I think: Felix Rodriguez, Adolfo Calero—

O'REILLY: Why do you keep talking about Central America?

GOODE: The world's not simple, Howie. O K? There's evil in it. And that evil is bigger and crueler and better organized than I ever figured it could be.

O'REILLY: Ollie?

GOODE: What?

O'REILLY: I'm on your side, remember? I'm scared, too.

GOODE: 'Too'?

O'REILLY: The hard part's admitting it.

GOODE: Suppose I was. Suppose I admit it. Then what? A weakness. It would be like begging you to grab my balls—

(GOODE *grabs* O'REILLY'*s balls.* O'REILLY *tries to get loose, but can't*)

O'REILLY: Cut it out, Ollie—

GOODE: And you know what, Howie? You would squeeze.

O'REILLY: No, I wouldn't—

GOODE: You'd squeeze until my balls cracked like eggs and the tears ran down my cheeks and I cried out for mercy, and you know why, Howie? You know why?

O'REILLY: Cut it out—!

GOODE: Because that is human nature.

(They are staring into one another's eyes. Again, O'REILLY *tries to get free, but can't. A beat.* GOODE *releases* O'REILLY.)

GOODE: There's a lot on these shoulders, Howie. They could burst in here. The kids with the machine guns? And that'd be it. 'Irish Tourists Murdered.' Who'd even notice? Or worse, they take us hostage.

O'REILLY: I know.

GOODE: You don't know. I know. Knowledge isn't power, it's dead weight. Tons of it.

O'REILLY: Share some of it. You're not alone.

GOODE: Technically. *(A beat)* If I ever spoke. Ever really spoke. The mountains that would move.

O'REILLY: You've done a lot, Ollie. Vietnam, all the decorations. Now the covert stuff. Grenada. The *Achille Lauro* caper. I admire you. You're what they used to call a hero, before people got too cynical to use the word anymore.

GOODE: I'm just one Marine.

O'REILLY: Not to the Old Man. He's counting on you.

GOODE: He once put his arm around my shoulder, Howie. The arm of the world's most powerful ruler. And I knew then what he wanted. Sometimes you have to rise above the written law. That's what he was saying to me with that arm. Get the job done, Soldier. And I thought, just for a second: I'm not worthy. I am just one man. Alone. (*He covers his face with his hands*) And I can't— By myself— It's too fucking much—!

(*He may or may not be sobbing. A beat, and* O'REILLY *reaches out a comforting hand to his shoulder. A beat, and* GOODE *grabs* O'REILLY's *wrist and twists it, cruelly*)

GOODE: I'm all right!

O'REILLY: Jesus, Ollie!

GOODE: You didn't see anything! You didn't hear anything! We didn't talk! We didn't even meet!

O'REILLY: All right!

(GOODE *lets go. A beat*)

O'REILLY: You need some sleep. You need it bad. (*He exits to the bedrooms*)

GOODE: They all want me to sleep. Why? What are they planning? Do oceans sleep? Do the planets relax their grip on the fate of man, and waste their power, dreaming? (*He is getting sleepy*) Sleep. Makes you soft, like warm down pillows. Alexander the Great and Rommel slept on straw mats. Two hours a night, maximum.

(*He starts to nod off... He is asleep. A beat. Suddenly, from behind the couch, stands* DAEMON. *She is dressed in a Marine officer's olive uniform that is too large for her, but her attire includes a feminine touch, such as high heels, so that the impression is one of someone having dressed up*)

DAEMON: Think of it, Ollie: If you had a hand-picked team.

GOODE: (*Snapping awake, staring wide-eyed, but without looking at her*) Not bureaucrats.

DAEMON: Guys.

GOODE: 'Nam vets.

DAEMON: No silk ties, no squash-court heroes.

GOODE: No "Let me check upstairs before I answer that, Ollie."

DAEMON: Realists.

GOODE: A twisted nose.

DAEMON: The silky scar of an old gunshot wound.

GOODE: We go through the streets of Tehran, disguised.

DAEMON: You head for the weak spots.

GOODE: People, seething with discontent.

DAEMON: Grown men fall weeping at your ankles.

GOODE: The tyranny of public mutilations. Baskets of cut-off hands.

DAEMON: You spread some money around, start a few fires.

GOODE: Show the people how, and pow! pow! the city's in flames.

DAEMON: We ship in the weapons.

GOODE: The people are up in arms, some arms have no hands.

DAEMON: We get a photo for the wire services.

GOODE: Young kid with clenched fist, though there's no fist.

DAEMON: World opinion is with us.

GOODE: I hand-pick someone neutral, a military man. He calls for U S advisers. We contact the Shah's brother in Palm Springs.

DAEMON: One problem, Ollie.

GOODE: What?

DAEMON: We don't know what the fuck we're talking about.

GOODE: Who *are* you?

DAEMON: Everything you fear and desire.

GOODE: How did you get in here?

DAEMON: Ivy League alumni clubs, summers on the Vineyard.

GOODE: State Department, right?

DAEMON: Cocktails at five, a driver at seven, the White House invitation list. A dedicated private secretary, the occasional blow-job at the end of hard work day. All that you desire but will never have. And I'm everything you fear. The other way of seeing it. Forgiveness. Heart. The courage to be innocent. I'm the little girl inside you.

GOODE: What do you want with me?

DAEMON: I'm here to protect you.

GOODE: From what?

DAEMON: Yourself.

GOODE: I'm following orders. We're redrawing the map of the Middle East.

DAEMON: You were never good at geography.

GOODE: I didn't ask for this. I answered a call—to serve my country. My president. (*A beat*). The silent luxury of the Oval Office at night. Every table lamp, a precious antique. In the hush of the inner sanctum, the Old Man drifts toward me. The impeccably tailored suit, the flash of a gold cuff link. I search for the words. "Mister President," I say, my voice breaking, "Sir, I would walk through fire. There isn't an ocean too deep, no mountainside that can keep, keep me from you—"

(*Enter* KELLY, *in pajamas*.)

KELLY: Ollie, for the love of Christ—

GOODE: (*Alarmed*) Chief, I don't know how she got in here!

(*A beat, as* KELLY *glances around for the absent "she"*)

KELLY: Pressure, Ollie. Sneaks up. Sleep's the key. And that's an order, Soldier. (*He exits.*)

DAEMON: I could read you a story.

(GOODE *looks heavenward for help. Lights fade. Music*)

DAY TWO, SCENE ONE

(*Morning.* O'NEILL *seated on the couch,* PADDY *leaning against the balcony glass door, his head on his forearm. Both men exhibit signs of exhaustion*)

O'NEILL: So what was it, do you think?

PADDY: I don't know.

O'NEILL: Well, think.

PADDY: I don't know. The lamb.

O'NEILL: The lamb? I ate the lamb—

PADDY: We can change subjects, yes?

O'NEILL: —but I didn't turn the bedroom into a toxic waste dump.

PADDY: I have a little gas.

O'NEILL: You have the North Sea. You have Prudhoe Bay.

PADDY: You woke me up.

O'NEILL: I couldn't breathe.

PADDY: That was the problem.

O'NEILL: You sleep out here tonight.

PADDY: Don't tell me what to do.

(Enter KELLY *from bedroom)*

O'NEILL: *(Cheerfully:)* Good morning, Chief.

*(*KELLY *does not respond. He takes a deep breath, holds a towel to his nose and mouth, and plunges into the bathroom)*

O'NEILL: What are you even doing here?

PADDY: Who?

O'NEILL: A Jew.

PADDY: Not so loud.

O'NEILL: Israeli agent.

PADDY: This room is bugged!

O'NEILL: Spying on us, right, Jew?

PADDY: *(Coming at him:)* Shut up!

O'NEILL: *(Retreating:)* A Jew in the middle of Muslim-land. They find out, your ass is hummus.

(They are nose to nose)

PADDY: I could crush you, insignificant bug.

O'NEILL: Why don't you just seal the doors and windows and fart me to death?

PADDY: I warn you. Control your mouth, Asshole.

O'NEILL: Control your asshole, Mouth.

PADDY: Hotel is dangerous place. You could have accident. A fall from balcony, for example.

O'NEILL: Don't try to intimidate me. You sleep out here tonight with Rambo.

PADDY: He doesn't sleep.

O'NEILL: You won't keep him awake, then.

(Enter GOODE, *carrying a modest-size black box: a satellite relay device. There is a phone receiver inside it. He proceeds to set it up on the coffee table)*

O'NEILL: (*To* GOODE) What was all the noise last night?

GOODE: What noise?

O'NEILL: Voices.

GOODE: You're hearing voices, maybe you need a little R & R.

O'NEILL: Don't you ever sleep?

GOODE: When?

O'NEILL: What's this? "Rambo, phone home"? You gonna tell them the truth? That the top Iranians won't come within ten miles of us, and this whole thing is going nowhere?

GOODE: Don't let them bluff you, O'Neill. I know a few things about the Arabs.

O'NEILL: They're not Arabs, they're Iranian. Persian ancestry.

GOODE: Technical detail.

PADDY: Not to Arabs.

O'NEILL: Or to the Iranians.

(KELLY *emerges, with towel, from the bathroom. He looks grim. He crosses downstage*)

KELLY: George.

(KELLY *gestures;* O'NEILL *joins him downstage*)

KELLY: Lot riding.

O'NEILL: Sir?

KELLY: On this. Eye, George. Keep one.

O'NEILL: Sir?

KELLY: On him.

O'NEILL: Who?

KELLY: O'Neill.

O'NEILL: I'm O'Neill.

KELLY: Ollie.

O'NEILL: Right.

KELLY: Counting on you, George.

O'NEILL: Yes, Sir.

KELLY: Screw-ups. Can't afford 'em. George?

O'NEILL: Sir.

KELLY: I like you. If I had a brother. Seriously.

O'NEILL: Thank you, Sir.

KELLY: Even when they'd come to me and say, "Bud. George?" I'd say, "Hey. Whoa."

O'NEILL: I appreciate it.

KELLY: Right to their faces. "Whoa."

O'NEILL: Thanks.

KELLY: With me? With me, Soldier?

O'NEILL: I don't have a hell of a lot of choice, do I?

KELLY: Good. Friends? O K?

O'NEILL: We'll see.

(KELLY *gives* O'NEILL *an awkward, manly-friendly pat*)

GOODE: Secure satellite relay ready to go, Sir.

(KELLY *approaches, takes the receiver from the box, and communicates, in a proper official and weighty tone*)

KELLY: Code: Operation Recovery. Update from Tehran, Monday, May 26, 1986, oh-eight-hundred hours. Dealing with fear, anxiety, paranoia, incompetence and stupidity.

(*A beat.* KELLY *surveys his colleagues. All exchange glances*)

GOODE: On *their* part.

KELLY: On their part, right. Armed guards in the hallways. Plumbing problem may be a deliberate attempt to wear us down. First arms transfer completed. No closure yet on American hostages, Beirut. They've promised us a new man for today, guaranteed high official. I've got some discouraged faces in this hotel room. But let me tell you, and them: a quitter never wins, and a winner never—

(A loud Beep! A recorded telephone operator's voice is heard)

VOICE: We're sorry, but to complete a national security satellite relay call, please enter your top-secret calling card number now. *(Beep!)* For international terrorism, press 1. For regional military conflicts, press 2. For domestic security, press 3—

*(*KELLY *hands the phone to* GOODE, *then exits to bedroom.* GOODE *hangs up, tries to re-dial. A knock at the door.* O'NEILL *opens it. A young Iranian man enters. He is* HIGH OFFICIAL, *although no one else knows it yet.)*

O'NEILL: Hold it right there. *(To his colleagues:)* Guys. Eggs and sausages all around?

PADDY: No sausage. Coffee.

O'NEILL: Right. No sausage for you. Four eggs and sausage, one eggs, big pot of coffee. And plenty of danish. You know what danish is? *(A beat)* Right. O K. *(He hands the man a dollar bill)* Now do you know what danish is, Ahmed?

*(*HIGH OFFICIAL *hands back the dollar bill)*

HIGH OFFICIAL: We don't want your money.

(A beat. GOODE *and* PADDY *approach.)*

GOODE: Who is this?

HIGH OFFICIAL: Allahu akbar.

GOODE: *(To* O'NEILL:) Translation.

O'NEILL: "God is great."

GOODE: Response.

O'NEILL: He certainly is?

GOODE: Ask him if he's the high official.

HIGH OFFICIAL: Why don't you ask me yourself?

GOODE: Are you? The high official?

HIGH OFFICIAL: The other two men were nothing. Now I am here. Through me you speak to the leaders of the revolution.

GOODE: (*To* PADDY) Get O'Neill.

O'NEILL: I'm O'Neill.

GOODE: The Chief, get the Chief! (*To* HIGH OFFICIAL:) You're willing to talk?

HIGH OFFICIAL: Everything you wish for, you may achieve. We stand on the brink of history. With God's help, we shall redraw the map of the Middle East.

GOODE: (*Calling:*) Bud! This is the real thing! Bud, get out here!

(*The door opens, and out strides* DAEMON)

DAEMON: Rein it in, Soldier. Maintain discipline, take a deep breath. Would you trust a man with a moustache like that? You know what they say, Ollie: When a deal looks too good to be true...it usually is.

(*Lights down. Music*)

DAY TWO, SCENE TWO

(A "briefing." GOODE, KELLY, PADDY, GHORBA, *and* HIGH
OFFICIAL, *several hours later. Maps and other documents
are spread across the coffee table.* HIGH OFFICIAL *is seated
on the couch, the others orbit around him, exchanging
glances, gesturing behind his back, etc. It becomes clear
that the Americans are improvising this "briefing."* GOODE
employs a retractable pointer for emphasis and precision)

GOODE: Your northeastern border.

KELLY: Infested.

GOODE: Your territorial waters, Caspian Sea.

KELLY: Their private pond.

GOODE: Your northwestern border.

KELLY: Crawling with Soviet "advisers".

PADDY: Ha!

GOODE: Only these advisers don't advise—

KELLY: They shoot.

GOODE: But your eastern border.

KELLY: Your eastern border.

PADDY: Ha!

KELLY: A joke.

PADDY: A debacle.

KELLY: Not even yours anymore. Ollie?

GOODE: Sir?

KELLY: Give him the numbers.

GOODE: The numbers?

PADDY: Not the numbers.

KELLY: The numbers.

PADDY: I protest.

KELLY: Protest denied.

GOODE: Sir— Just give them?

PADDY: Toss like fish?

GOODE: These are not just numbers—

PADDY: Diamonds. Solid gold.

GOODE: The balance of power in the Middle East.

(*A beat*)

KELLY: Give him the numbers.

GOODE: (*Reluctantly*) Six Soviet infantry divisions. Four tank divisions.

PADDY: Eight.

GOODE: Right, eight infantry.

PADDY: No, eight tank.

GOODE: Eight tank?

PADDY: And six infantry.

GOODE: That's what I said.

HIGH OFFICIAL: Gentlemen. The current numbers are seven Soviet infantry, nine tank.

KELLY: What are your sources?

HIGH OFFICIAL: The Afghanis.

GOODE: Unreliable.

PADDY: Horse thieves and murderers.

KELLY: You'd believe an Afghani dope-smoker over a multi-billion dollar reconnaissance satellite?

GOODE: The point is, what are the Soviets doing massed at your border?

HIGH OFFICIAL: Fighting a war against the Afghans.

PADDY: For now.

KELLY: What about tomorrow?

PADDY: Or next week?

GOODE: A warm-water port.

KELLY: Been after one since Peter the Great.

HIGH OFFICIAL: They have the Black Sea.

PADDY: Access to the Persian Gulf.

HIGH OFFICIAL: They have Iraq.

KELLY: Don't underestimate the Soviets.

PADDY: They are ruthless.

GOODE: These are people who will stare you in the eye and lie to your face.

HIGH OFFICIAL: Question, please.

GOODE: Shoot.

HIGH OFFICIAL: (*To* PADDY:) You have an odd accent for an American.

PADDY: No, I don't.

GOODE: No, he doesn't.

HIGH OFFICIAL: Where are you from?

(PADDY *and* GOODE *speak the next lines simultaneously.*)

PADDY: Florida.

GOODE: Brooklyn.

KELLY: Point is, protection.

GOODE: Territorial integrity.

KELLY: Help you maintain it.

HIGH OFFICIAL: This is generous of you.

KELLY: Tell him about Vladimir.

PADDY: I protest!

GOODE: Chief—

KELLY: Tell him.

GOODE: Top-ranking Soviet general.

PADDY: In our pockets.

GOODE: Author of this: (*He produces an anonymous looking document.*) "The Invasion of Iran."

HIGH OFFICIAL: May I see it?

KELLY: Not so fast.

GOODE: Let's talk a little quid pro quo.

HIGH OFFICIAL: What is the quid?

GOODE: The quid?

HIGH OFFICIAL: The quid.

PADDY: What's the quo?

GOODE: Before we show you our quid, let's see your quo.

KELLY: Let's talk turkey.

HIGH OFFICIAL: What does Turkey have to do with us?

GOODE: No, no—

HIGH OFFICIAL: Turkey is neutral country. Islamic, too.

KELLY: Look. We help save your asses from the Soviets, you release our people.

HIGH OFFICIAL: For the sake of argument: suppose the Soviet danger is not so great.

GOODE: Not so great?

PADDY: Ha!

HIGH OFFICIAL: Afghanistan is their Vietnam. And then there is the new guy.

KELLY: The new guy?

HIGH OFFICIAL: Gorbachev. Things could change.

PADDY: "Change"?

GOODE: Look at me. Right here. Things will not change.
O K?

(HIGH OFFICIAL *reaches over and takes the document that*
GOODE *has left carelessly on the table.*)

GOODE: Hey, that's classified!

HIGH OFFICIAL: The pages are empty.

GOODE: No, they're not.

HIGH OFFICIAL: Blank pages. (*He shows them, then tosses
the document back on the table. A beat*)

KELLY: 'Course they're blank.

GOODE: That's right.

KELLY: Think we'd bring the actual plans with us?

PADDY: What do we look like to you, idiots?

(*A beat. They stare at* HIGH OFFICIAL.)

HIGH OFFICIAL: Must I answer?

GOODE: The point is, you need us.

PADDY: More than you think.

HIGH OFFICIAL: Why then have you come to us?

KELLY: You invited us.

HIGH OFFICIAL: We didn't invite you.

GOODE: Yes, you did.

HIGH OFFICIAL: Who told you this?

(*All eyes turn to* GHORBA, *who is picking his nails. A
double-take when he sees they are staring.*)

GHORBA: My friends, what I said was—

GOODE: Shut up!

HIGH OFFICIAL: Shut up! (*A beat*) There is the matter of
the missile parts.

KELLY: First, the hostages.

HIGH OFFICIAL: But we have paid already for parts, and tank shells. You promised to bring everything with you.

GOODE: No, we didn't.

HIGH OFFICIAL: You did.

KELLY: Who told you that?

(*All eyes to* GHORBA)

GHORBA: The truth of the matter is—

HIGH OFFICIAL: Shut up!

KELLY: Shut up!

HIGH OFFICIAL: (*To* KELLY:) You wish to save us from Soviets? Deliver what we paid for.

GOODE: We will.

KELLY: We will. You have my word.

HIGH OFFICIAL: When?

GOODE: As soon as the American hostages are freed.

HIGH OFFICIAL: The hostages?

GOODE: They're in your control.

HIGH OFFICIAL: Who told you this? No, never mind. The hostages will be freed. You have my word.

KELLY: When?

HIGH OFFICIAL: As soon as you deliver the arms.

GHORBA: My friends—

GOODE: Shut up!

HIGH OFFICIAL: Shut up!

KELLY: (*To* HIGH OFFICIAL:) Who are you, anyway? Don't even know who we're talking with.

GHORBA: He is high official.

PADDY: How high?

GHORBA: High above you, Mister Assistant.

KELLY: Give you priceless intelligence information—

GOODE: You scoff at it—

KELLY: Reveal our top-secret Soviet source, Alexei—

GOODE: "Vladimir."

KELLY: Vladimir, and you barely blink—

GOODE: We've got our doubts about you, Mister.

KELLY: I want a minister.

GOODE: We were promised ministers.

KELLY: I am a minister.

GOODE: He's higher than a minister.

HIGH OFFICIAL: You come here in secret, like thieves, with false passports. You want official meeting, make official visit.

(*A beat*)

KELLY: (*Preparing to leave*) O K, that's it. Pulling the plug.

GOODE: (*To* HIGH OFFICIAL:) Now look what you did.

KELLY: Leaving. Right now. That's it. Kiss this historic opportunity good-bye.

(*A beat. No one moves*)

HIGH OFFICIAL: So leave.

KELLY: No.

GOODE: Lives are at stake.

KELLY: Give you a second chance.

GOODE: Free our hostages.

HIGH OFFICIAL: How many?

KELLY: All four.

HIGH OFFICIAL: Simple thing. Americans are freed, they all come home. Television cameras, international news. You will be heroes.

GOODE: What's the timetable?

HIGH OFFICIAL: Simple. First deliver arms. (*He stands.*) As gesture of good faith, I have for you a gift. (*He withdraws items from his pocket, tosses them on the table.*) Your Irish passports.

(*Lights to black. Irish music*)

DAY TWO, SCENE THREE

(GHORBA, GOODE. *Same setting, three hours later.* GHORBA *is showing* GOODE *the pages of a glossy magazine.*)

GHORBA: And this one. (*A beat*) Ah. And this one. (*He gives a low whistle*) Hah?

GOODE: (*He gives a low whistle*) Woo. Nice.

GHORBA: No. Not nice. Gorgeous. She waters your mouth, no? Here. What you could do with this. No? You are a man?

GOODE: What? Yes—

GHORBA: Of course you are a man. Women know this of you. Here, look. Swedish.

GOODE: Oh God...

GHORBA: You will curl up at night, this baby in your arms. You see this here? Look!

GOODE: I see it.

GHORBA: She could be here. Now. Tonight.

GOODE: Tonight?

GHORBA: Ollie. Give in to your desire.

GOODE: I can't.

GHORBA: You must!

GOODE: Here? Now? Are you crazy?

GHORBA: You want it. You need it. Ollie: look!

(GHORBA *again shows* GOODE *the magazine. A beat*)

GOODE: (*Giving in*) All right.

GHORBA: Ah!

GOODE: If—

GHORBA: What?

GOODE: You throw in the ammo.

GHORBA: Free? With beautiful gun like this? Hey, want to see really cute tank? Chinese. Super discount.

GOODE: Ghorba, when they get out, there'll be a parade in every town in America.

GHORBA: Baker's dozen. You have thirteenth tank half-price.

GOODE: "The hostages are free." They'll shout it from the church steeples. The whole country will kneel in prayer.

GHORBA: Free ship to Honduras.

GOODE: But I don't want the glory. Let the bureaucrats like him cash in. He'll get his book contract. A run for the Senate. Not this Marine. When they do the press conference in the Rose Garden, where do you think I'll be?

GHORBA: Managua?

GOODE: Behind a column on the White House portico, just another soldier who served his president. Oh, word'll leak out eventually. "Sorry, Mister Rather. I can't comment directly, Sir. I can only say, God was with me every step of the way." (*A beat*) They've been in there three hours. I don't want any last-minute screw-ups.

(The bedroom door opens. KELLY *appears. He seems very tense)*

KELLY: Get. In here. *(He exits. The door closes)*

GOODE: If he fouls it up now— I need those hostages.

GHORBA: So send here now all of American weapons you promise.

GOODE: I told you: hostages first, then the hardware.

GHORBA: When you tell me?

GOODE: From the beginning.

GHORBA: I never hear this.

GOODE: Ghorba! Dammit!

GHORBA: Khomeini not accept this never.

GOODE: When did you talk to Khomeini?

GHORBA: He is to me close like this.

GOODE: You want your cut, you get me those hostages.

GHORBA: Hah! Money. I am people person.

GOODE: The hostages are people.

GHORBA: Khomeini is more important people.

GOODE: Cross me on this and I'll have your ass.

GHORBA: You make threat at me, Mister Big Spy? I know how you charge Iran triple price for weapons.

GOODE: And I know about your two million dollar "commission".

GHORBA: And I know where goes this triple money, Mister Wheeler-Dealer. *Buenas dias, amigo. Bienvenida a Nicaragua.*

(The bedroom door opens again.)

KELLY: Ollie, dammit, I want you in here. Now. (*He returns to the bedroom, the door closes.*)

GHORBA: You don't like deal, go home. Maybe you walk back to America. Revolution Guards want your plane.

(*Exit* GHORBA. GOODE *stands for a moment in contemplation.*)

GOODE: The situation looked bleak. Many men would have given in to despair.

VOICE: (*From behind the curtain*) But not this Marine, right?

(*The curtains are flung back and* DAEMON *emerges. She is dressed as a hostage: hair disheveled, ragged clothes, chains around her ankles and running to her wrists, so that she moves and gestures with difficulty.*)

DAEMON: Face it, Ollie. We're cooked.

GOODE: I'll work it out.

DAEMON: Hardware for human flesh.

GOODE: We have to do something.

DAEMON: What if they only trade two? Or just one? Who'll decide?

GOODE: I don't know.

DAEMON: All or none. Your President's orders.

GOODE: So we compromise.

DAEMON: With human lives? You're in over your head.

GOODE: I can handle it.

DAEMON: But can the hostages? You know, I was thinking.

GOODE: Will you get out of here?

DAEMON: If I were a Hezbollah in Beirut—

GOODE: Just leave me alone.

DAEMON: And the Americans were offering weapons—

GOODE: I'm trying to think—

DAEMON: I'd turn in my hostages.

GOODE: Exactly. See?

DAEMON: Then I'd go out and kidnap me a couple more.

GOODE: No!

(The bedroom door opens abruptly and out stride KELLY *and* HIGH OFFICIAL.)

HIGH OFFICIAL: It's all settled.

KELLY: It's not settled.

HIGH OFFICIAL: Just meet a few conditions and you can have all your hostages.

GOODE: We'll meet them. What are they?

KELLY: Stay out of this, Ollie.

HIGH OFFICIAL: Simple thing. Israel withdraws from southern Lebanon and Golan Heights—

GOODE: Israel?

HIGH OFFICIAL: —Kuwait frees all the Da'wa prisoners—

GOODE: Kuwait?

HIGH OFFICIAL: And America pays Hezbollah expenses.

GOODE: What expenses?

HIGH OFFICIAL: For taking and keeping hostages. (*A beat*) Here, we take short break. (*He moves to the exit.*) You really should do something about the stench in here. (*He exits.*)

KELLY: "We've got it all worked out, Bud." "It's a historic opportunity, Bud." "We'll redraw the map of the Middle East, Bud." (*He exits to bedroom.*)

DAEMON: (*To* KELLY *exiting:*) It's not his fault. All he knows about foreign affairs he learned in a rice paddy in Vietnam.

GOODE: Will you shut up!?

DAEMON: As the sun sets in Beirut, it rises on the barrios of Managua.

GOODE: I had to do *something*. Men, being tortured. Soldiers, dying. Can't you see that?

(*Exit* GOODE, *to hallway.*)

DAEMON: (*Calling after him:*) We've created a monster, Ollie. Now we have to keep it from biting you on the bottom! (*A beat. To the audience:*) He means well. His heart is in the right place. But then, the problem's not his heart...

(*From behind the balcony curtain, where he has been listening to everything,* O'NEILL *emerges. He enters one of the bedrooms, closing the door behind him.*)

DAEMON: But soft: the enemy is everywhere. Time passes. Expectations crumble. Darkness descends.

(*The* HIGH OFFICIAL *enters stealthily. He does not see* DAEMON. *She slips out as he enters.*)

(*Alone in the room,* HIGH OFFICIAL *moves to the couch. He is holding something wrapped in a handkerchief. Swiftly he places it under the couch. As he does so,* O'REILLY *emerges from the bathroom, towel over mouth and nose.* HIGH OFFICIAL *makes an effort to appear as if all is normal*)

HIGH OFFICIAL: Allahu akbar. They would be unhappy with you. Your bosses.

O'REILLY: Why?

HIGH OFFICIAL: Leaving me alone here. I might be a spy.

O'REILLY: I'm not feeling well.

HIGH OFFICIAL: Your first visit to Iran?

O'REILLY: I think it was the tap water.

HIGH OFFICIAL: I had the same thing once in Florida.

O'REILLY: (*With glance toward the bedroom*) They've been in there for hours.

HIGH OFFICIAL: I see you as different from the others. More open, no?

O'REILLY: Me?

HIGH OFFICIAL: Even curious. About us.

O'REILLY: I'd love to get out, see the city.

HIGH OFFICIAL: I can arrange this.

O'REILLY: Talk to the people.

HIGH OFFICIAL: Certain people, yes.

O'REILLY: That's how you learn things.

HIGH OFFICIAL: Precisely. Ask questions.

O'REILLY: Here's one.

HIGH OFFICIAL: Yes?

O'REILLY: What are you hiding under the couch?

HIGH OFFICIAL: What couch?

O'REILLY: Pick it up, nice and slow.

(HIGH OFFICIAL *slowly removes the object from its hiding place, holds it in his hand for* O'REILLY *to examine.*)

O'REILLY: Chocolate cake?

HIGH OFFICIAL: Would you like a bite?

O'REILLY: I thought it was Ramadan.

HIGH OFFICIAL: The temptations of the Great Satan.

(O'REILLY *and* HIGH OFFICIAL *eat.*)

O'REILLY: So. You're a realist.

HIGH OFFICIAL: When I need to be. Idealism is also very real. Especially during a revolution.

O'REILLY: Where were you? Harvard?

HIGH OFFICIAL: Princeton.

O'REILLY: Don't they mistrust you?

HIGH OFFICIAL: Of course.

O'REILLY: Was he really that awful? The Shah?

HIGH OFFICIAL: A businessman. Much as you have now on Wall Street.

O'REILLY: No wonder you had a revolution. (*A beat*) You're religious?

HIGH OFFICIAL: I? Certainly.

O'REILLY: You have to be.

HIGH OFFICIAL: It's safer, yes. But I believe. You're familiar with Islam?

O'REILLY: Sure. Well, I'm reading some books. As background.

HIGH OFFICIAL: Forgive me, but your colleagues are weak on background, no?

O'REILLY: Islam they find a little mysterious. They're real sharp on Communism, though.

HIGH OFFICIAL: You would do well to learn about us quickly. Islam's future is richer even than our past. Remember, we too were once a world power, when Europe was still in the Dark Ages.

O'REILLY: Why do you hate us? Americans, I mean?

HIGH OFFICIAL: Don't believe all the rhetoric. Rhetoric is for us a weapon. And we have so few.

O'REILLY: You could have lots more, if you learned to trust us a little.

HIGH OFFICIAL: A man was traveling with Mohammed. When they came to a village for the night, he asked Mohammed, "Should I tether my camel, or trust to God?" Mohammed answered, "Trust to God—and tether your camel." Why do you fear us so?

O'REILLY: Maybe it's because you're so different.

HIGH OFFICIAL: But our countries have much in common. For example: We proudly base our politics on religion. No false separation, church and state. I notice, under Reagan, you begin to do the same.

O'REILLY: So Khomeini is, what? Like a saint?

HIGH OFFICIAL: There are no saints in Islam.

O'REILLY: But you worship him.

HIGH OFFICIAL: Admire. Only Allah is worshipped.

O'REILLY: How many times a day do you pray?

HIGH OFFICIAL: Sunrise, noon, afternoon, evening, night.

O'REILLY: I pray once a week. Half an hour, in church.

HIGH OFFICIAL: Then you go home and mow the lawn.

O'REILLY: Not if I can help it. Golf, more likely. So show me.

HIGH OFFICIAL: What?

O'REILLY: How it's done. There's a ritual, right?

HIGH OFFICIAL: You really want me to show you?

O'REILLY: You face east?

HIGH OFFICIAL: Toward Mecca and the kaaba.

O'REILLY: You have to have a prayer rug?

HIGH OFFICIAL: No, just a clean spot. The muezzin sounds the call to prayer.

O'REILLY: From the minaret.

HIGH OFFICIAL: That's right. He chants the shahada. "*Allahu akbar...*" Take off your shoes. Here, stand next to me.

(O'REILLY *does so.*)

HIGH OFFICIAL: These are the rakatin, the different prayer positions. Now, right hand over left hand, like this. (*He places his hands on his chest*) Now this.

(HIGH OFFICIAL *and* O'REILLY *go through the ritual of traditional prayer.* HIGH OFFICIAL *bends, putting his hands on his knees.* O'REILLY *follows his movements: he kneels, with hands on his thighs*)

O'REILLY: They say you can feel the power of it.

HIGH OFFICIAL: Islamic prayer?

O'REILLY: That it's a transcendent experience.

(HIGH OFFICIAL *leans forward and touches his head to the floor.* O'REILLY *mimics the movement. The two men remain in this last position a moment. Enter* GOODE.)

GOODE: Howie! Jesus Christ!

HIGH OFFICIAL: Wrong god, my friend.

O'REILLY: (*Standing*) He was just demonstrating.

GOODE: Praying with the enemy?

HIGH OFFICIAL: Am I your enemy?

O'REILLY: Ollie, relax.

GOODE: We've got Americans held prisoner—

O'REILLY: I know.

GOODE: And you're praying with a Moslem?

O'REILLY: It's all the same God.

GOODE: I don't buy that. Why doesn't he pray for the hostages? Or how about setting them free?

HIGH OFFICIAL: Who will set you free?

GOODE: What is that, a riddle? Huh?

O'REILLY: Ollie, why don't you try to get some sleep?

GOODE: And while I'm asleep, he converts my men?

O'REILLY: "Your" men?

HIGH OFFICIAL: The real hostage is you.

GOODE: You know, I've about had it with you.

HIGH OFFICIAL: You believe the lie of your own power.

GOODE: We're not powerful?

HIGH OFFICIAL: Helpless to save four of your own people.

GOODE: You think we couldn't do it?

HIGH OFFICIAL: You come begging to us—

GOODE: Diplomacy, not begging.

HIGH OFFICIAL: —a poor, Islamic country. But we have God, and justice.

GOODE: What about the hands?

HIGH OFFICIAL: What hands?

GOODE: Chopped off for stealing? That's justice?

HIGH OFFICIAL: Your death rows, full of black men—

GOODE: They have all their hands on death row, Pal.

HIGH OFFICIAL: Your society, paralyzed with fear—

GOODE: Your top people, afraid to talk to us—

HIGH OFFICIAL: You come here as Irish. Who is afraid?

GOODE: This country, it's primitive out there—

HIGH OFFICIAL: Trading arms for human lives, what is more primitive?

GOODE: A nation of fanatics—

HIGH OFFICIAL: Born-again Christians!

GOODE: Even your damn bathrooms don't work.

HIGH OFFICIAL: Our belief in God makes bathrooms irrelevant!

O'REILLY: Ollie, it doesn't hurt to see it from their perspective.

GOODE: Keep out of this.

HIGH OFFICIAL: "Do they say, 'We are a victorious army'? Their army shall be routed and put to flight." The Holy Koran, Moon, 54:44.

GOODE: You want to start quoting?

O'REILLY: Ollie—

(They circle one another, like boxers, and hurl their Biblical-Koranic quotes)

GOODE: "He that hath no sword, let him sell his garment, and buy one." Luke, 22:36.

HIGH OFFICIAL: "Prophet, make war on the unbelievers and the hypocrites..." Repentence, 9:73.

GOODE: "An hypocrite with his mouth destroyeth his neighbor." Proverbs, 11:9.

HIGH OFFICIAL: "Who does greater evil than he who lies against God?"

GOODE: "By their fruits ye shall know them."

HIGH OFFICIAL: "The man or woman guilty of theft, cut off their hands..."

GOODE: "If thy right eye offend thee, pluck it out."

HIGH OFFICIAL: "Let evil be rewarded with like evil."

GOODE: "An eye for an eye."

HIGH OFFICIAL: "You shall drink boiling water—!"

GOODE: "A tooth for a tooth!"

HIGH OFFICIAL: "—You shall drink it as the thirsty camel drinks!"

(A beat; he's searching.)

GOODE: "Consider the lillies of the field!"

HIGH OFFICIAL: "...a monstrous blasphemy is that which they utter!"

GOODE: "Give us this day our daily bread!"

HIGH OFFICIAL: "God is great!"

GOODE: "Glory to God in the highest!"

HIGH OFFICIAL: "He is the Mighty, the Wise One!"

GOODE: "Let my people go!"

(The bedroom door opens suddenly, and KELLY appears. He is disheveled and unsteady.)

KELLY: I had a dream. Horrible. Howie.

O'REILLY: Sir?

KELLY: The Oval Office. News photographers. The Old Man. "I accept Bud's resignation—" And the handshake. *(Staring at his hand:)* But I didn't have— There wasn't any—

O'REILLY: Yes, Sir.

KELLY: Cut off.

O'REILLY: Just a dream, Sir.

KELLY: Howie.

O'REILLY: Sir.

KELLY: Where are we?

(Lights to black. Music)

DAY TWO, SCENE FOUR

(*A few hours later.* HIGH OFFICIAL, GHORBA, GOODE *and*
KELLY. *Negotiations continue*)

GOODE: Two?

HIGH OFFICIAL: Two.

KELLY: You're saying two?

HIGH OFFICIAL: Two.

GOODE: Two.

KELLY: Which two?

HIGH OFFICIAL: (*Shrugs*) Two.

GOODE: When?

HIGH OFFICIAL: Soon.

KELLY: How soon?

HIGH OFFICIAL: Soon.

GHORBA: Two American lives. You will be heroes.
Maybe even senator, Bud.

KELLY: Don't—

GHORBA: O K.

KELLY: —ever call me Bud.

GHORBA: O K.

KELLY: Ever.

GOODE: What are the conditions?

HIGH OFFICIAL: None.

KELLY: I have your word on that?

HIGH OFFICIAL: Of course.

GOODE: No conditions.

HIGH OFFICIAL: None. (*A beat*) Except ones already
agreed.

KELLY: We didn't agree!

GHORBA: (*To* HIGH OFFICIAL:) You can't be serious about those demands.

HIGH OFFICIAL: But they don't know that.

KELLY: Hey, hey.

GOODE: Whoa, whoa.

KELLY: Let's keep it English.

GOODE: Open and honest, O K?

GHORBA: (*To the Americans:*) Just chit-chat. (*To* HIGH OFFICIAL:) You don't have the hostages, do you?

HIGH OFFICIAL: Not exactly.

GHORBA: Do you even know who does?

(GOODE *and* KELLY *confer, aside*)

GOODE: Two. That's good.

KELLY: "Good"?

GOODE: We take what we can get, then push for more.

KELLY: Orders. President himself. All or nothing.

GOODE: Go back empty-handed?

KELLY: How do we even know two?

GOODE: We try it.

KELLY: They don't control the prisoners.

GOODE: How do we know?

KELLY: We can't trust them.

GOODE: We take a chance.

KELLY: No.

GOODE: Human lives, Bud.

KELLY: We have orders.

GOODE: American flesh, it's worth *any* risk.

KELLY: I said no.

GOODE: I don't fail missions—

KELLY: You heard me, Ollie.

GOODE: I find a way. I fight and kick and bite until I find a way.

KELLY: No.

GOODE: We're taking the two.

KELLY: I'm in charge here—

GOODE: You fuck this up, Bud—

KELLY: That's an order, Soldier.

GOODE: And you'll take the hit for it.

(A beat)

HIGH OFFICIAL: *(To* GHORBA*:)* Divided they fall.

GHORBA: You're playing a dangerous game.

HIGH OFFICIAL: Just relax.

GHORBA: Fifteen million worth of beautiful weaponry.

HIGH OFFICIAL: You told me the price was seventeen.

GHORBA: Seventeen, right. That's what I just said.

HIGH OFFICIAL: Who's playing the dangerous game? *(To the Americans:)* My friends. I have good news. The captors have given in. Israel may remain in the Golan Heights.

KELLY: What about the hostages' expenses?

HIGH OFFICIAL: My government will pay this. But you must work to free the prisoners in Kuwait.

GOODE: We will, we'll work on it.

KELLY: No guarantees. We can't control what a foreign government does.

HIGH OFFICIAL: You mean to say you don't control these Moslem prisoners?

KELLY: No.

HIGH OFFICIAL: And yet this is what you expect from me—control of the American prisoners. We have no choice but to trust one another.

GOODE: Who has the hostages?

HIGH OFFICIAL: Does it matter?

KELLY: How do we know they won't change their demands again?

HIGH OFFICIAL: You don't. I suggest you act quickly.

GOODE: We'll take the two.

KELLY: All four or none.

GOODE: Two now, and we talk on the others.

KELLY: You located the two?

HIGH OFFICIAL: Of course.

KELLY: Then release them.

HIGH OFFICIAL: All right.

KELLY: Now.

HIGH OFFICIAL: It is done. (*A beat*) When you release the weapons.

KELLY: (*To* GOODE:) See that?

GOODE: We expected people first, then the arms.

GHORBA: And we expect arms first, then the people.

HIGH OFFICIAL: Time is running out.

GOODE: For God's sake, Bud—

KELLY: No.

HIGH OFFICIAL: The weapons are on a plane. Let this plane take off. If the hostages are not in your possession by noon, call back this plane.

GOODE: It's doable, Bud.

KELLY: No.

HIGH OFFICIAL: You have my word this will work.

KELLY: No word. Release all the hostages. Then you'll have your weapons.

GHORBA: It is very complicating—

KELLY: So uncomplicate it.

GOODE: Bud, dammit—

KELLY: No. That's it. (*He exits.*)

HIGH OFFICIAL: There is an American phrase, what is it? "End run." A going-around, yes? (*A beat*) You know what I really want, Ollie? What I dream of? American roast beef.

GHORBA: With gravy.

HIGH OFFICIAL: Yes, gravy.

(*Lights down. Music*)

DAY TWO, SCENE FIVE

(*Lights low. It is late night and the hotel suite looks deserted. Enter DAEMON. She is dressed as a hostage, as before: leg irons, hands chained, etc. She shuffles downstage center and addresses the audience. Her brave attempts at gesture are foiled by her chains*)

DAEMON: Say what you want. Criticize him. Vilify him. But he's focused on the human element, the innocent victims. It's up here, and in here. He cares. He does. He wants to get his arms around them, bring them back home, but it's complicated, the foreign part of foreign policy, he wants to break free and do the heroic thing, but his hands are tied, he's chained to a way of thinking. Help him. He's a prisoner!

(Enter KELLY, in pajamas. Is he sleepwalking? Or praying?)

KELLY: God. My God. Please. Don't let me fuck this one up, too. *(He leans against the wall next to the bathroom door)* Their cold stares and murdering silence. They see I'm struggling, they watch me suffer. "Mister President. Fellow cabinet members. The mission... The mission, Sir... was a failure. A total and complete—"

(The bathroom door bursts open, slamming into KELLY behind it. GOODE appears, breathing deeply)

GOODE: I have an order. The order is wrong. I *know* it's wrong!

(He crosses to the balcony, steps outside. The bathroom door swings slowly back and KELLY collapses to the floor, unconscious. Enter, from the hallway, HIGH OFFICIAL, followed closely by GHORBA)

HIGH OFFICIAL: Children. I am dealing with children.

GHORBA: So push them. Threaten them.

HIGH OFFICIAL: They could be hostages. All of them. Easily.

GHORBA: But we have a business deal—!

HIGH OFFICIAL: If this fails...

GHORBA: My money—

HIGH OFFICIAL: Your *neck*, Mister Too-Close-to-the-C I A. *(He exits.)*

GHORBA: *(Following him)* I hardly know them. I visited once, in Langley. As a tourist, basically.

(Exit GHORBA. Enter O'REILLY and O'NEILL, from the bedroom)

O'NEILL: I'm warning you, Howie. I've been turning over some rocks, just to see what crawls out. Here, read this.

(O'NEILL *hands* O'REILLY GOODE's *notebook.*)

O'REILLY: I don't want to see it.

O'NEILL: I am seven years, eleven months and twenty-six days from a full pension.

O'REILLY: You stole that.

O'NEILL: This thing is gonna blow. The pieces are gonna land on *our* heads.

O'REILLY: You stole it.

O'NEILL: Confiscated. As a defensive measure.

(O'NEILL *and* O'REILLY *exit to hallway. Enter* GOODE *from balcony.*)

GOODE: It's wrong, you know it's wrong. What do you do?

DAEMON: Sleep, Ollie. Three nights without sleep.

GOODE: Christians held by Moslems. Nobody dares to say that? (*A beat*) Where's my notebook? Who took my notebook!?

(*Exit* GOODE *to left bedroom. Re-enter from hallway* O'REILLY *and* O'NEILL.)

O'NEILL: It's some Central America angle. I don't know what it is—yet.

O'REILLY: George, we're a team.

O'NEILL: Of individuals.

O'REILLY: We hang together. When the going gets tough—

O'NEILL: The tough get indicted.

O'REILLY: You coward.

O'NEILL: A coward with a job. And a pension.

(O'NEILL *and* O'REILLY *exit to right bedroom. Enter* PADDY *from hallway, followed by* GHORBA)

PADDY: One hostage, ten hostage: public relations. Five hundred tank shells—*that* is foreign policy.

GHORBA: So push them, threaten them. If I lose my cut, you lose yours. Remember this.

PADDY: I have done all I can do.

GHORBA: I have friends, with guns, in lobby. If they find out a Jew is in here...

PADDY: And if they find out Iranian arms dealer is Israeli double-agent...

GHORBA: I deny it!

(*Exit to hallway* PADDY, *followed by* GHORBA. *Re-enter* GOODE)

GOODE: I release the plane. By the time he finds out, the hostages are free.

DAEMON: Your mind is confused.

GOODE: The deal's done. Everybody wins.

DAEMON: Sleep, Ollie.

GOODE: The map of the Middle East is redrawn. Flags fly from every church steeple. Unless— Something goes wrong. (*A beat*) An empty stage. The auditorium is packed: senators, congressmen, reporters with graduate degrees from good colleges. I stand naked in the wings. I try to dress, but men with dark glasses are hurrying me. They push me on stage. "Wait!" I cry. "My pants!" I stumble forward. The lights blind me. I can hear their laughter. "Ladies and Gentlemen, please, I wasn't ready—!" I try to cover my nakedness, but I can't— I trip and fall to the stage— Striding toward me from the wings— His eyes flashing with rage— Mister President, please, I can explain—! (*A beat*) I'm sorry!!

(*During his speech,* GHORBA *and* PADDY *have entered from the bedroom.* PADDY *carries a black box: the satellite relay communication device*)

PADDY: Ollie. Let it go.

GHORBA: The plane.

PADDY: Release it.

GHORBA: Who will know?

PADDY: You're a take-charge guy.

(PADDY *places the box next to* GOODE.)

GHORBA: A man.

PADDY: Take charge.

GHORBA: One little order.

PADDY: History.

GHORBA: Profit.

PADDY: Innocent victims.

GHORBA: *Amigos valientes de Nicaragua.*

(GOODE *removes the receiver from the box. A strange light glows from within the box. We hear the sound of ringing. Someone picks up. A voice is heard. It sounds remarkably like that of former President Ronald Reagan.*)

VOICE: Yes, who is it? Hello? You'll have to speak up, I can't hear too well out of this ear. Hello? Hello? Hello?

(*Lights fade. Music*)

DAY THREE, SCENE ONE

(*Dawn.* O'NEILL *and* O'REILLY, *in full tourist array. They have just returned from eating*)

O'NEILL: God. The stewed lamb. Huh?

O'REILLY: Yeah.

O'NEILL: Glorious. And the curry fish? Whoa.

O'REILLY: Right.

O'NEILL: Great religion. Fast all day, stuff yourself all night, feel closer to God.

O'REILLY: All the war casualties everywhere. It almost made me sick.

O'NEILL: You gotta hand it to them: fresh seafood in the middle of a war.

O'REILLY: Kids with their legs blown off, not even 16 years old.

O'NEILL: Caviar! Red caviar for that kind of money?

O'REILLY: Zero money for you.

O'NEILL: I'll pay you back.

O'REILLY: Right. Like Geneva.

O'NEILL: I still owe you for Geneva?

O'REILLY: You think I don't know that move?

O'NEILL: What move?

O'REILLY: The waiter shows up and poof.

O'NEILL: What?

O'REILLY: Off to the men's room. You're famous for it.

O'NEILL: Who?

O'REILLY: You haven't picked up a check since they overthrew Allende.

O'NEILL: You know, I am sick of working with you.

O'REILLY: When did you ever 'work'?

O'NEILL: Always whining. Total liberal.

O'REILLY: I'm a liberal?

O'NEILL: Talking to the locals, asking questions. Great way to blow our cover.

O'REILLY: I told them I was Irish.

O'NEILL: Sucking up to Bud.

O'REILLY: "Sucking up"?

O'NEILL: Getting chummy with what's-his-face.

O'REILLY: Who?

O'NEILL: "Show me how to pray." What, are you writing a book?

O'REILLY: You are such an asshole, you know that?

O'NEILL: You're the asshole.

O'REILLY: You don't know anything about them.

O'NEILL: You're the asshole.

O'REILLY: Nothing human, just dates and stats.

O'NEILL: That's right, Asshole.

O'REILLY: Don't call me that.

O'NEILL: O K, Asshole.

(O'REILLY *wrestles* O'NEILL. *It is an awkward and pathetic effort on both parts, two bureaucrats fully unprepared for physical combat. In the midst of battle,* O'NEILL *grips his back and cries out in pain.*)

O'NEILL: What are you, crazy?

O'REILLY: I'm sorry—

O'NEILL: Didn't you know about my disc problems?

O'REILLY: Here, sit down—

O'NEILL: Keep away from me, you maniac. I'm filing a complaint. If I go on sick leave again, your ass is in a sling.

(Enter KELLY from the bedroom.)

KELLY: Time. No one woke me?

O'REILLY: Ollie was supposed to.

KELLY: Matter with George?

O'NEILL: I've been physically assaulted, that's all.

KELLY: *(Alarmed)* The Guards? Are they coming back?

O'REILLY: It wasn't the Guards, Sir.

O'NEILL: It was Mister Sucker Punch here.

KELLY: Howie?

O'REILLY: I lost my temper, Sir.

KELLY: Well, dammit, I will not tolerate that!

O'NEILL: I'm filing a complaint. This happened on your watch, Bud.

KELLY: *My* watch? I was asleep.

O'NEILL: We all know what you do in your sleep— strangler!

KELLY: That's a lie! Ask my wife!

(Exit O'NEILL, painfully, to bedroom, followed by KELLY.)

(Enter GHORBA from hallway, with an open bottle of champagne. He pauses at the door, and takes a music hall stance. As he begins to sing, in marches GOODE, with plastic cup. He joins in the song)

GHORBA: You. Are. A...

GOODE & GHORBA: *(Singing)*
Grand old flag, you're a high flyin' flag
Da-da-DAH, Da-da-DAH, da-da-DAH!
The land I love, the land I love,

The home of the free and the brave!
Every heart beats true for the red, white and blue—
May old acquaintance be forgot
Keep your eye on the grand ol' flag!

GHORBA: Howie, I may present to you: The Man... Who Brought Home Hostages!

O'REILLY: Ollie. You did it?

GOODE: Damn straight, Howie!

GHORBA: Two down. Two to go down.

GOODE: "I'm sorry, Mister Rather, I can't comment directly, Sir. All I know is: God was with me every step of the way!"

O'REILLY: Which two? Who are they?

GOODE: Don't know yet.

GHORBA: Coming is confirmation.

O'REILLY: Ollie, this is huge! This is front-page!

GOODE: I did it, I did it, I knew I could do it!

GHORBA: Yes, yes, yes!

GOODE: You take *action*, Howie. Two countries are talking again. Trade first, then understanding. Who knows where we go from here. The Ayatollah at Camp David? You think big, big things come to pass.

O'REILLY: Can I say something totally off the wall? (*A beat*) Who's gonna play you in the movie!?

(*Whoops, laughter, high-fives, etc*)

(*Enter* KELLY *from the bedroom.*)

KELLY: Howie. Packing up, moving out. Fifteen minutes.

GOODE: Negative, Bud. We've got a breakthrough.

GHORBA: Two hostage. Free at noon, this day.

KELLY: Heard that before.

GOODE: For real this time, Bud.

GHORBA: All night we are working. Two Americans, Bud.

KELLY: Don't call me Bud. Howie. Pack it up.

GOODE: We can't leave now.

GHORBA: Five hours more, Bud.

GOODE: We're *this* close.

GHORBA: You will be heroes.

KELLY: Orders. All four or nothing.

GOODE: Listen to me, Bud—

KELLY: Get your hands off me.

GHORBA: Two now. The plane, it comes, and two maybe tonight.

KELLY: What plane? Ollie.

GHORBA: We have business deal.

KELLY: Is that plane in the air?

GOODE: No.

KELLY: You launch it, Ollie?

GOODE: No.

KELLY: No authority, launch that plane.

GOODE: I didn't.

KELLY: Don't lie to me.

GOODE: I'm not.

KELLY: Swear to God?

GOODE: Yes.

(*A beat. The two men stare at one another.*)

GOODE: Let it land, Bud! Two American lives—!

KELLY: Gave you an order.

GOODE: My president wants his hostages, dammit!

KELLY: You don't know what he wants—

GOODE: He's counting on me!

KELLY: Howie. Call back that plane.

GOODE: You're a loser, Bud. The President knows it. He told me so himself.

KELLY: Howie.

GOODE: "Ollie," he said. "Bud's got to go. He's a weight around my neck."

KELLY: Howie.

GOODE: You're on the way out, Loser.

O'REILLY: Yes, Sir.

KELLY: Call it back.

GOODE: Howie, wait. Twelve more minutes and the plane's past the refuel point.

KELLY: Howie.

GOODE: Two American lives!

KELLY: That's an order.

GOODE: You're signing their death warrants!

GHORBA: My friends, let us nicely sit and have discussion—

KELLY: Shut up!

GOODE: Shut up!

KELLY: Howie.

GOODE: Eleven minutes.

KELLY: Your career. On the line.

GOODE: Two human beings.

KELLY: Up for promotion next month.

GOODE: They've been tortured.

KELLY: Walk into that room.

GOODE: Don't do it, Howie.

KELLY: Call back the plane.

GOODE: He'll drag you down with him!

KELLY: Then pack your bags.

GOODE: He assaulted his own wife! In bed! Arrest him, Howie.

O'REILLY: What?

GOODE: I'm taking over. You're relieved of command, Bud.

KELLY: Don't listen, Howie.

GOODE: I'm in charge now. Arrest him.

O'REILLY: Me?

KELLY: Big mistake, Howie.

GOODE: Disarm him.

O'REILLY: He's not armed.

GOODE: Take his pills.

KELLY: Howie. Promoting you. Second-in-command.

GOODE: Don't listen to him.

KELLY: Congratulations, Howie.

GOODE: It's a trick!

KELLY: You're what, a GS-14?

GOODE: Howie, listen: a foreign post, somewhere warm.

KELLY: Ever work on a senate campaign, Howie? I could use you.

GOODE: Costa Rica in January, it's heaven.

KELLY: Last chance, Howie. Call back that plane—now.

GOODE: Howie, have the balls to say no! Howie!

(GOODE *has grabbed* O'REILLY *by the private parts. A beat.* O'REILLY *frees himself and exits to bedroom*)

GHORBA: This is message you give to Iran? Cheating, lying?

KELLY: Americans obey orders.

GHORBA: We ordered weapons. Where are these?

KELLY: Safest policy, Ollie.

GOODE: Do you realize what you've done?

KELLY: You'll thank me for this.

(GOODE *begins to advance on* KELLY; KELLY *retreats.*)

GOODE: Two human lives. On your head.

KELLY: Did what we had to do.

GOODE: You fucking candy-ass!

KELLY: Maintain discipline.

GOODE: You Beltway bureaucrat!

KELLY: Close ranks. United we stand.

GOODE: This is real! This is human flesh, red meat, life and death, not some fucking numbers in the President's popularity poll!

KELLY: I order you to shut up!

GOODE: This is Beirut and Moscow and Central America! I'm into shit even you don't know about!

KELLY: You're confined to quarters! Go to your room!

(GOODE *and* KELLY *are face to face. A beat. They go for each other's throat. A brief moment of violent but ineffectual strangulation*)

GHORBA: Choke him, Ollie! Choke him!

(*Enter* HIGH OFFICIAL)

HIGH OFFICIAL: Gentlemen, please! Gentlemen!

(The combatants straighten up, try to restore an air of dignity.)

HIGH OFFICIAL: Congratulations. You have triumphed. *(He reads from a piece of paper.)* Hostage Number One: Laurence Martin Jenco. Number Two: Thomas Sutherland. At noon. After delivery of weapons.

KELLY: No deal.

HIGH OFFICIAL: No what?

KELLY: Leaving in ten minutes.

HIGH OFFICIAL: We have your people.

KELLY: All four or none.

HIGH OFFICIAL: This is absurd.

KELLY: Orders from our president.

HIGH OFFICIAL: He orders you to refuse two hostages? Think about this.

KELLY: We obey. No thinking.

HIGH OFFICIAL: Ollie.

KELLY: I'm in charge.

HIGH OFFICIAL: All night we work. Now we send them back?

KELLY: Let them out, humanitarian gesture—

HIGH OFFICIAL: Where is yours?

KELLY: —we get the other two, you get the arms. My word.

HIGH OFFICIAL: Your word is worthless.

GHORBA: Not worthless even.

HIGH OFFICIAL: Your own hostages can't trust you. Why should I?

(Exit KELLY to bedroom.)

HIGH OFFICIAL: Americans. You treat all foreign people like customers. You know everything, so there is nothing to learn. (*Waving the paper*) Two lives. Your own people. All or nothing? (*He crumples the paper and tosses it to the floor.*) Nothing. (*He exits.*)

GHORBA: Ollie. I have friends in hallway, with rifle. We hold this Bud, downstairs in parking garage—

(*Enter* KELLY, O'REILLY, O'NEILL, *with suitcases.* O'REILLY *carries* O'NEILL'*s. The latter limps. They cross to the door*)

O'NEILL: Get a lawyer, Howie. You, too, Bud. This whole fiasco is going to wind up in court.

GHORBA: Bud, my friend, still you can fix this big mistake—

O'NEILL: I've been assaulted because *I* know what's really going on around here.

(*He halts, facing* GOODE, *and tosses him his notebook. Exit* O'NEILL *and* O'REILLY)

GHORBA: Bud, think of quarter-million dollar cash, on your kitchen table, your wife, laughing—

KELLY: (*Ignoring* GHORBA) Better snap to it, Ollie. (*He exits.*)

GHORBA: (*Calling after him:*) I am businessman, treat me with business ethics! This is all I ask you! (*To* GOODE:) You owe me seventeen million dollars. (*As he exits:*) Bud! My friend, wait! (*He exits.*)

GOODE: The map of the Middle East: unchanged. My spirits were rock-bottom. I thought of the Americans in Beirut, their families back home, and my heart ached.

(*Enter* DAEMON, *dressed in a cliché of Arabic robes, something out of T E Lawrence.*)

DAEMON: Free yourself, Ollie.

GOODE: The politicians, that's who did it.

DAEMON: Admit your failure.

GOODE: They got scared and bailed out.

DAEMON: One God, one truth?

GOODE: You can't trust them.

DAEMON: What if everything you know is wrong?

GOODE: One God, one truth.

DAEMON: New ways of seeing.

GOODE: Belief is a strength.

DAEMON: And a chain.

GOODE: They're counting on me.

DAEMON: Embrace your ignorance.

GOODE: The hostages. The Contras. My president.

DAEMON: Pray, Ollie. Ask for enlightenment. Get on your knees.

(GOODE *does so.*)

DAEMON: A new god.

GOODE: No.

DAEMON: For a new world.

GOODE: Things. Will not change.

DAEMON: Don't be afraid. Begin to imagine: all that you don't know. Eight hundred million believers. Feel their strength. Make their power yours.

(GOODE *lowers his head to the floor. Re-enter* KELLY.)

KELLY: Can't find my, uh—

GOODE: (*Rising up*) Here I am, O Lord!!

(*The two men freeze. A beat.* GOODE *scrambles to his feet.*)

KELLY: (*Searching his pockets*) Good, long rest, Ollie. Back home.

GOODE: You blew it, Bud.

KELLY: Politics. Can't take it personally.

GOODE: American lives!

KELLY: Casualties. Foreign policy has 'em.

GOODE: How can you say that?

KELLY: Did our best. Honest effort.

GOODE: I have one more shot to fire.

KELLY: Put it behind us. No hard feelings.

GOODE: The Ayatollah's seventeen million.

KELLY: Ah. Found 'em. (*He takes a vial of pills from his pocket. As he speaks the next few lines, he tries to open the vial and shake out a pill.*)

GOODE: We diverted it.

KELLY: What?

GOODE: The money. It went to the Contras in Nicaragua.

(KELLY *freezes. A beat*)

KELLY: Didn't hear that. Don't know this.

GOODE: Iran to Switzerland to Costa Rica.

KELLY: Never learned of it. Didn't approve it.

GOODE: We had to act, Bud.

KELLY: "We"? Illegal. Congressional ban.

GOODE: They need guns, and bullets. They're fighting for survival!

KELLY: (*He has a pill*) Survival's what you don't know and can't be blamed for. Didn't fail here. 'Cause we never came here. (*He puts the pill in his mouth, then looks at the vial in his hand.*) Aagh!! (*He spits out the pill, coughs, chokes.*) Oh God! Suicide pill—! Thought it was my Valium—! Oh God!! (*He exits.*)

DAEMON: God is merciful.

GOODE: We were *this* close.

DAEMON: The press is not.

GOODE: I should've just acted on my own.

DAEMON: They'll find out now.

GOODE: No way. Top secret.

DAEMON: "If three men talk in secret together, Allah is their fourth." There are no secrets, Ollie. You are lunch meat, Soldier.

GOODE: Not this Marine.

DAEMON: Deli roast beef.

GOODE: I did my duty.

DAEMON: They'll serve you up to the wolves.

GOODE: I met the enemy—

DAEMON: And he is in Washington. What's crueler: no hands or no future?

(GOODE *grabs* DAEMON.)

GOODE: You know so much, tell me this: How do I get rid of you?

(DAEMON *grabs* GOODE.)

DAEMON: I'm with you all the way—to the top or the bottom. Without me, you won't know the difference. (*Her grip on him becomes tender now*) Ollie. Don't fight me. Learn to love me.

GOODE: You want me to show a weakness.

DAEMON: You're going to need me now, more than ever.

GOODE: I did what I had to do. I believe. In my country, in my God, the Lord Jesus Christ.

DAEMON: Another true believer.

GOODE: I believe in fighting and dying for what I believe in.

DAEMON: A Christian Jihad!

GOODE: The more I see of the world, the more I know: We are right.

DAEMON: And righteous, too.

GOODE: There are plenty who don't believe that.

DAEMON: The infidels are everywhere.

GOODE: And I'll get to them before they get to me. One truth. That's all I need.

(DAEMON *brings* GOODE *his Marine dress uniform jacket; she helps him into it.*)

DAEMON: But *which* truth, Ollie?

(*Sounds of a gavel are heard*)

DAEMON: That's the real battle—and it's about to begin.

(*Again, gavel sounds*)

DAEMON: Don't be afraid. I'm here.

(GOODE *and* DAEMON *are downstage now, in a pool of light. The sounds of a Senate hearing room. A gavel bangs three times.*)

SENATOR: (*V O*) Swear in the next witness.

SENATE AIDE: (*V O*) Raise your right hand.

(GOODE *and* DAEMON *raise their hands.*)

SENATE AIDE: (*V O*) Do you swear to tell the truth, the whole truth, and nothing but the truth, so help you God?

(GOODE *and* DAEMON *glance at one another.*)

GOODE: I do.

(*A final, loud gavel sound. Lights fade on* GOODE. *A spot on* DAEMON, *who comes downstage and speaks to us*)

DAEMON: (*She picks up the piece of paper that* HIGH OFFICIAL *threw to the floor moments ago; opens it; shows it to us:*) Blank. (*She prays:*) Hear me, O Lord: Protect us from the men who would remake the world in your name, for our own good. (*To us:*) We live in an age of true believers. The truest believers rule. Is there no place left for the doubters? Here, upon a stage—one place, at least, where there is still room for doubt. Ah, but that's all one. Our history play is done. And we strive to please you, every day.

(DAEMON *bows. Lights to black*)

END OF PLAY

www.ingramcontent.com/pod-product-compliance
Lightning Source LLC
Chambersburg PA
CBHW070020110426

42741CB00034B/2258

9780881454314